Making Light Work

Making Light Work

*An End to Toil in the
Twenty-First Century*

David A. Spencer

polity

First published in 2022 by Polity Press

Polity Press
65 Bridge Street
Cambridge CB2 1UR, UK

Polity Press
101 Station Landing
Suite 300
Medford, MA 02155, USA

ISBN-13: 978-1-5095-4862-0
ISBN-13: 978-1-5095-4863-7 (pb)

A catalogue record for this book is available from the British Library.

Library of Congress Control Number: 2021941123

Typeset in 11 on 13 pt Sabon by
Cheshire Typesetting Ltd, Cuddington, Cheshire
Printed and bound in Great Britain by CPI Group (UK) Ltd, Croydon

For further information on Polity, visit our website:
politybooks.com

For Deborah, Polly and Florence

Contents

Acknowledgements

This book has benefitted from the inputs of a number of people. I would like to thank the following who contributed to the ideas in the book with conversations, comments and advice: Andrew Brown, John Budd, Felix Fitzroy, Robert Skidelsky and Gary Slater.

I have gained from working with Matt Cole, Chris Forde, Simon Joyce, Chris McLachlan, Mark Stuart and Xanthe Whittaker on different research projects and from participating in the ESRC Digital Futures at Work Research Centre.

I wrote this book while Head of the Economics Division at Leeds University Business School. Thanks to colleagues in the Division and School for their support.

I would also like to thank the students I have taught. Those on my third-year undergraduate module 'The Political Economy of Work' have proved a particular source of insight and inspiration. I am grateful to be in a position where I can teach ideas that derive from my own research and for the opportunity to engage with such great students.

George Owers at Polity provided important encouragement and constructive criticism throughout all stages of the book. The comments of three anonymous reviewers were also helpful in improving the contents of the book. Fiona Sewell provided valuable copy-editing.

Finally, I would like to thank my wife, Deborah, and my daughters, Polly and Florence. The book has meant long periods of self-isolation and some personal struggle. Thank you, Deborah, Polly and Florence, for always being there and for lightening my life.

1

Introduction

I don't like work – no man does – but I like what is in the
work – the chance to find yourself. Your own reality –
for yourself not for others – what no other man can ever
know. They can only see the mere show, and never can tell
what it really means.

Joseph Conrad, *Heart of Darkness* (1899)

Work, work, work

Work is an obligation that very few of us can avoid. Work
is what we do to earn wages. It provides the means for us
to live. In modern society, we cannot escape work without
facing some material hardship. The lack of work is associated with distress mainly because it is linked to the loss of
income. Most of us work, in this respect, because we have
to, not because we necessarily want to.

But work is also an activity that means something to us.
We value certain aspects of the work we do and sometimes
work longer than we need to. While many of us lament the
time work takes and the restrictions it places on our lives,
we also find reasons to keep working that are independent

of the income that work brings. Work has a hold over us, even while it remains something we have to perform.

Various examples confirm this fact. Lottery winners keep on working when they can afford to stop. John Doherty, from Renfrewshire, Scotland, won a £14m lottery jackpot in 2016, but decided to continue his job as a plumber. Asked why he wanted to continue working despite having the money not to, he replied that he would be bored staying at home and did not want to let down his loyal customers.[1]

Those nearing retirement worry about the prospect of not working. Indeed, many retired people miss their former jobs and often seek a return to paid work. In addition, many people volunteer to work in their communities – tasks that attract payment in the formal economy are undertaken for free. Finally, the unemployed strive to work for reasons beyond the need for income.

The positive features of work encompass not just the opportunity to interact socially but also the scope to develop and use valued skills and to gain self-esteem. Work matters because it offers the potential for activity that enables us to be and do things in our lives that we value. We work for pay, but we also seek other things in work that add to our well-being.

Of course, in reality, work often falls short of our expectations and needs. Work can be – and frequently is – a burden and source of pain in itself. Its costs extend not just to the lack of opportunity for progress in work but also to the exposure to mind-numbing work activities. We rightly deplore sweatshops not only because they are linked to chronic low pay but also because they are associated with harsh and life-limiting work conditions. The deprivations of work, in this case, challenge our views about what work should be like.

Money matters, again, to the extent that it can buy us freedom from bad work. The richer a person is, the less likely she is to work in a sweatshop. The benefit of a lottery win is that it buys us the freedom to quit our present jobs if we dislike or hate them. But winning the lottery also creates the potential to undertake different and more pleasurable work – it appeals to the idea of working better, not quitting work altogether.[2] For some retired people, with the safety net of a pension, there is the option to choose work that is satisfying – perhaps to a greater extent than the kinds that were undertaken before retirement.

Nonetheless, beyond money, all of us have a craving and need for work that matches with our potential and meets our innermost desires. Our participation in voluntary work indicates how we desire work for intrinsic reasons. Indeed, voluntary work may offer compensation for the lack of enjoyment we derive from paid work. Unemployment, too, for all its material costs, is harmful partly because it deprives us of the opportunity to gain the direct benefits of work. Some of the fear associated with unemployment derives from a concern about the negative experience of a life without work.

Work, in short, has meaning in itself. In the present, it might be undertaken to pay the bills and service outstanding debt. But it is also an activity that shapes us – for good and for ill – and it remains an activity that we care about, even when it does not necessarily allow us to live well.

This book is concerned with the different roles that work can, does and should play in human life. In the book, I reflect on how modern work, in its myriad forms, prevents well-being. I am clear that work is a problem in contemporary society. I support the argument that work is harmful to the lives of many people. I also actively support the view that work exerts a too dominant influence in human life and that we should strive, as a society, to work less. I back, for example, the case for a shorter working week – the reduction of work time should be a key demand of a progressive society. Yet, at the same time, I argue that work should be changed. The possibility of changing work – of lightening it, in a quantitative and qualitative sense – lies at the heart of this book and inspires the critical arguments made in support of reform in society.

The book engages with ideas from past and present literatures on work. The account is not necessarily exhaustive (e.g. it largely ignores consideration of forms of unpaid work). But it is, hopefully, useful and instructive in setting out some key areas of debate and controversy in the study of work. A distinctive aspect is the attention given to the costs as well as benefits of work, not as contingent features, but as system-wide outcomes. I make the point that capitalism, as a system, creates alienating forms of work. At the same time, however, I argue for change in the system of work, not just to negate alienation linked to work, but also to create the conditions for non-alienating work in the future. The goal of creating a different future of work – one where work is human, as opposed to an alienating activity – drives the arguments in the book.

Here I seek inspiration in the writings of some prominent critical thinkers, notably Karl Marx and William Morris. Marx's ideas on the alienation of work under capitalism are relatively well known – however, as I will argue, his broader vision of negating work alienation and of returning meaning to work in a post-capitalist future have tended to be overlooked in debate, including in some radical circles. An aim of this book is to restate and revive this vision as part of a broader critical analysis of work.

William Morris – the nineteenth-century artist and socialist – is much less well known than Marx. Yet his writings on the costs of work and on the possibilities for recreating work beyond capitalism match with those of Marx. Indeed, Morris's own thoughts on the present and future of society were directly inspired by Marx. I will draw on Morris's ideas to show the scope for transforming work and creating a future society where meaning as well as pleasure can be returned to work.

Politically, the book sides with arguments that seek radical change. I argue against the view that capitalism is the end of history or the best of all possible systems. Instead, I put forward the argument for a world beyond capitalism. Following Marx and Morris, I see capitalism as a barrier, not just to more time away from work, but also to more rewarding and meaningful work. The agenda for change which the book supports aims to secure a society that enables everyone not only to work fewer hours, but also to work better. I argue that such a society cannot be realized while capitalism remains in place, and that a new system will be required to bring forth the forms of work and life that are compatible with wider goals of economic sustainability and human flourishing.

In writing this book, I am conscious of a number of recent books on the subject of work. These range from general histories of work (the idea and activity) through to direct critiques of work.[3] Prominent in critical discourse are perspectives promoting a 'post-work' politics. These perspectives side with the view that work should be rejected and ultimately eliminated. They also feed broader narratives about the need to secure a post-capitalist future – one where we work as little as possible and enjoy our lives with a minimal exposure to work.[4]

Interest in work has also been fuelled by new debate on the progress of technology and the possibilities for automation. Several books now predict that work for wages will decline in the future.[5] This decline is linked to rapid and seemingly unstoppable advances in new digital technologies. For some, there is the prospect of a 'world without work'. This prospect is met with both fear and hope and is used to support alternative policy proposals. For example, it has led to calls for a 'universal basic income' (UBI) and a four-day work week.

I address critically contributions to the post-work literature as well as to the modern debate on automation and the future of work. I take an opposing position. In terms of post-work ideas, I argue for the transformation of work, as opposed to its negation. The idea of negating work betrays a lack of imagination about how work can be recreated in the future. On the topic of automation, I debate whether society would be better or worse off by using technology to replace human labour. Here I suggest that a progressive case for reform must embrace the goal of putting technology to use in reducing work hours while enhancing the quality of work. In this case, moves can and should be made to achieve both less and better work.

There are other notable aspects of the book. One aspect relates to the coverage of ideas. Given my background as an economist, there will be references to the economics literature. This reflects partly on how economics has influenced the wider understanding of work – in particular, economics has helped to promote an understanding of work as an instrumental activity that is performed mainly for money. Economics has also presented work as a cost and sought to elevate the benefits of higher consumption – in this respect, it has embedded an ideology in support of higher economic growth. I will take issue with this way of thinking about work and will point to the need to look beyond economics in understanding the meaning and role of work. Given my wider concern for interdisciplinary research, there will also be an integration of ideas from different disciplines and subject areas. Broadly, the book can be seen as a contribution to the development of a political economy approach to the study of work.

In a previous book, I developed ideas towards a political economy of work – in particular, I examined how ideas about work had evolved and changed in economics, both past and present.[6] The present book pushes the debate a stage further, by examining how work might be studied differently and reimagined in the future.

This book is written at a time of crisis, not only of work, but of society in general. This crisis has been created by COVID-19. To be sure, work was not working for the majority before the onset of the pandemic. In the UK as well as the US, for example, problems of in-work poverty have coincided with issues of unequal pay and long work hours. But COVID-19 has magnified and deepened the problems of work, in part by adding to unemployment, but also by increasing workloads and creating new dangers for those in work. So-called 'key workers' (e.g. in health services) have felt particular pressure, being required to work excessive hours and under conditions that present direct harms to their health.

I recognize that COVID-19 has hit some groups more than others – minorities, for example, have faced a higher death toll, partly because of their exposure to jobs in which risks of harm have been higher. Women, too, have faced higher burdens of work (both unpaid and paid). The pandemic has revealed starkly the inequities in society and the unfitness of the present capitalist system as a means to meet our collective and individual needs.[7]

But I will suggest through the pages of this book that a different future can and must be created. Contemporary debates focus on 'building back better' – creating a better, more robust future.[8] These debates can have a hollow ring, in the sense that they can cloak a call for the restoration of the same system that existed before COVID-19 struck – one that left society exposed to the pandemic once it hit. Rather, my argument is that the crisis must be a moment for critical reflection on the present and future of society – that is, it should lead us to question the current order of things and to build a different system where we can all live and work in ways that not only protect our health, but also enable us to carry out activities (including in work) that bring meaning and pleasure to our lives.

In promoting alternatives beyond the crisis, this book supports the idea and goal of lightening work. I argue that the crisis linked to COVID-19 has shown how work must be shared out in society and how lighter work for all is a laudable and potentially achievable goal. But I also argue that the crisis reminds us of how work should be improved upon in qualitative terms. We need to discuss what essential work is and how it is to be directed and organized in our workplaces. In essence, if a better future of work and life is to be achieved, then we must make strides to lighten work, in terms of both the hours it occupies in the day and the quality of experience it offers in our lives. This book, then, seeks to promote the lightening of work as a specific political demand.

The ideas in the book are outlined across several chapters. Chapter 2 examines different meanings of work. Here I highlight the error of seeing work as perpetually bad or good and instead argue for a more nuanced approach that links the costs and benefits of work activities to the actual system of work. In advancing this argument, I invoke the ideas of Marx and Morris, including those on the scope for reclaiming work as a creative and pleasurable activity. Their vision of transforming work into something positive in human life is one I endorse. Indeed, this vision inspires ideas in the rest of the book.

Chapter 3 asks why work hours have stayed long under capitalism and why the quantitative lightening of work has remained elusive. Focusing on J. M. Keynes's famous 1930 essay, 'Economic Possibilities for Our Grandchildren', I examine the barriers to, and benefits of, working less. I defend the argument that work hours should be reduced in society and promote the vision of a future where shorter work hours add to the quality of work and life.

Chapter 4 discusses some realities of modern work. I assess critically David Graeber's 'bullshit jobs' thesis and evaluate other approaches that defend and criticize work in society. This discussion culminates in support for an objective definition of the quality of work. I focus on how the nature and system of work can limit workers' ability to meet their needs, and I emphasize the importance of structural reform in delivering higher-quality work.

Chapter 5 asks whether high-quality work can be made available to all. I show how some economic and ethical arguments endorse the restriction of high-quality work to a minority in society – in effect, contending that society should accept the inevitability of a world where some people (perhaps even the majority) do low-quality work. I refute these arguments. Instead, I build a case for extending to all workers the opportunity for high-quality work.

Chapter 6 examines modern debate on the possibilities for automation and labour-saving technology. This debate is increasingly influential in shaping opinions about the future of work – indeed, it has led to predictions of the demise of work. I strike a sceptical note, pointing out limits to automation in the present. I also highlight how notions of automation have been linked to understandings of the meaning of work and how these notions have driven alternative agendas for change (some more radical than others). I argue that the modern debate on automation needs to tackle issues of ownership if it is to see the full potential for changing work in the future.

Chapter 7 examines issues of policy and politics. I raise questions in relation to current growth-based policies, the objective of full employment and the implementation of a UBI. Instead, I set out an alternative reform agenda. The latter encompasses support for a four-day work week, but also returns to ideas found in Marx and Morris on the requirement to change the nature of work. Change here includes shifts in the goals of work as well as in the ownership of workplaces. The vision of work transformation drives the reform agenda I propose.

Chapter 8 sets out the key conclusions and contributions of the book. In particular, it reiterates how less and better work can be realized jointly in a society beyond capitalism. I also reflect on how, given the occurrence of repeated crises, change has become a much more urgent and necessary task – one that we should seek to promote and help to bring into being. Visions of 'building back better', I conclude, are only credible if they include a direct commitment to reduce work hours while securing work tasks that are meaningful and pleasurable in themselves.

2
Meanings of Work

All true Work is sacred.
Thomas Carlyle, Past and Present (1843)

All of us do work, whether we like it or not. Work fills our time, our heads and our discussions about life. It defines who we are and who we are able to become. It affects our standing in society and our ability to live comfortably. It also creates pleasure for some and outright hostility for others.

But while we might take for granted the forms that work takes and bemoan or celebrate its character, the meaning of work has evolved through time. Work for wages, for example, only exists because of the presence of capitalism. The definition of ourselves through work also relies on certain ideas about what work means in society. These ideas have been subject to change and have drawn strength from wider beliefs about the role of work in economic reproduction and in the formation of human character.

Importantly, too, there has been controversy and dispute about the meanings attached to work. For some writers, work has appeared as just 'work' – an activity done for its material ends. Yet for others, work has been an activity with wider meaning and importance. Several critical writers, indeed, have seen in work the basis for a better life and the recreation of society. Political agendas for change have included a direct focus on work and have linked goals of freedom and justice to progress in the content and experience of work.

In this chapter, I focus on some influential ideas that have addressed the meanings of work. These ideas push in different directions, contesting work as well as praising it. They are also linked to specific ideologies about what form work should take. I highlight, in particular, views that see work as a curse and as a virtue. These views are associated with disparate thought, from economics to religion. I argue that they remain deficient in seeing work as all bad or all good – what they miss is the link between the system of work and the character of work itself and how change in the meaning of work is possible (and indeed necessary). In developing this argument, I draw on the idea of alienation (linked to the writings of Marx) and show how this idea can be used to develop a different understanding of work, both as it exists under capitalism and as it might exist in a future society. I also draw insight from the writings of William Morris.

The curse of work

The conception of work as something irksome and loathsome in itself has a long history. The ancient Greeks and Romans, for example, saw little value and benefit in work.[1] They preached the virtues of a life where work was absent. 'Free' people led good lives by avoiding work, not embracing it. Work was imposed by necessity and was to be allocated to slaves. The indignity of work was reflected in the lack of freedom suffered by slaves, and happiness was equated with a life free from manual labour. Plato and Aristotle were able to fulfil their creative potential, precisely because they had time on their hands to do as they pleased. In the realm of politics, the ability to write about and participate in democracy derived from the freedom not to work. Here high principles of democratic freedom clashed with the realities of a strict social hierarchy that condemned large numbers of people to slavery and enforced manual labour.

Early Christian thought repeated the same negative depiction of work. Because of Adam's indiscretion in the Garden of Eden, humans were condemned to live out their years on Earth labouring for a living. The fate of mankind was to earn their bread by the sweat of their brow.[2] Those who read the Bible were not given much hope of ever enjoying the work they did. Rather, they were instructed to see it as a mere means of survival. Work itself remained a pain that all humans had to endure.

It is worth noting that the origins of the costs of work were seen as universal. To the ancient Greeks, work had no redeeming quality, but rather remained a task that was, in its nature, painful. In early Christian thought, the costs of work were God-given – they reflected the Fall of Man. This way of defining work cast an ideological shadow – in particular, it lent credence to the idea that work was to be accepted as a pain, rather than challenged as such. Because it was in the nature of things that work was a hated activity, workers were to accept their lot and put up with the burdens they were born to endure. Such views, therefore, undermined the case for reforms aimed at improving the nature of work.

Later writers carried forward the focus on work's inherent costs. In 1706, the English philosopher John Locke argued that work for its own sake was 'against nature'.[3] Humans worked not because they wanted to, but rather because they had to. Only biological needs drove humans to work. It was implied that humans would avoid all work if they could and that human happiness was associated with a no-work state. The possibility of attaining this state was ruled out, of course, by the fact that mankind had to work in order to meet their immediate needs.

Early economic writers – linked to mercantilist doctrine – promoted the view that work was a curse, but added to this the idea that workers were lazy.[4] Prominent in the seventeenth and early eighteenth century, these writers complained about workers' slothfulness. English workers were seen as too lazy and too insolent to deliver the work required to raise national wealth.[5] The only cure for the 'labour problem', as the mercantilists saw it, was the perpetuation of poverty. Mercantilism, in this way, became associated with the 'utility of poverty' thesis – the belief that a more productive and compliant workforce depended on reducing wages to subsistence level.

Mercantilist writers such as Thomas Mun showed no sympathy for the plight of workers. While society had evolved beyond slavery, there was still a view that workers occupied a place at the bottom of the social order. Workers were born to labour. Indeed, they were born to labour on behalf of the nation. A nationalistic appeal to the merits of hard work was used by the mercantilists to justify poverty for the masses. Workers might not benefit directly from working hard, but it was their duty to work in order that the nation could become richer.

Allied to this view was the idea that work offered a distraction from vice. Work might not be good in itself – indeed, it was recognized to be a painful undertaking – but it offered a way to avoid the drunkenness, debauchery and riot that would come from workers having too much time on their hands. The great concern of the mercantilists was that workers – free from the obligation of work – would act immorally and without regard to the national interest. Despite its intrinsic costs, work at least provided a basis for virtuous behaviour and national economic success. In this case, work was to be enforced on workers – for their own good.[6]

Here the mercantilists took no account of how work was evolving in society and how changes in the character of work (particularly the shift to wage-labour) were resisted by workers not for reasons of lethargy and sloth, but because of the commitment to previously established patterns of working. Workers in England were accustomed to working irregularly and with some autonomy.[7] The mercantilists, however, represented – through their arguments and protestations – a new pattern of work, based on continuous working and extended hours. The move to wage-labour was also associated with more arduous and harsh working conditions – ones that held few attractions for workers.[8] Faced with these changes and conditions, it was no wonder that workers used whatever extra income they could obtain to work less. But this resistance reflected a desire for relative freedom. In short, mercantilism failed to see how workers' resistance to work was not given by their nature, but rather was influenced by their concern to cling on to ways of working and living that were threatened by the emergent system of wage-labour.

Politically, the mercantilists were not unbiased in their views – rather, as members of the privileged classes, they had vested interests in portraying all workers as incorrigibly lazy, because it gave a justification for pushing down wages. The fact that the mercantilists' views were subject to bias means that we can challenge their credibility as a basis for understanding how and why work was resisted at the time they wrote. Generally, though, mercantilist labour doctrine shows us how ideas about work can be mobilized – in a negative way – to justify the costs of work and how these ideas can become a direct barrier to its reform.

The classical economists that followed the mercantilists challenged the idea that poverty was required to induce workers to work – rather, taking the position that poverty was a barrier to higher productivity, they sided with moves to raise workers' wages.[9] Adam Smith, notably, supported higher wages on economic as well as moral grounds. Workers were more likely to work hard if they were paid higher wages.[10] And society was more likely to be harmonious and happy if the majority in society were free from poverty.[11] The continuous increase in wages, in Smith's view, was the key to economic prosperity and social stability.[12]

But Smith, with other classical economists, continued to endorse the idea that work was an innate pain. He, again along with other classical economists, also continued to view workers as lazy. Higher wages were justified, in part, to provoke workers into working. The 'carrot' of higher wages replaced the 'stick' of poverty; however, the view remained that workers had to be goaded to work and that workers' preferred life-state was one of unlimited ease or rest. The concern was to maintain some kind of 'optimal' wage that was not so high as to give workers the option of not working and not so low as to make them unable to meet their needs.[13]

On work itself, Smith offered a clear definition – work was all 'toil and trouble'.[14] For him, there was no merit in work beyond its contribution to wealth creation. Workers would not just sacrifice their free time in working; they would also experience pain in the activity of work itself. Though Smith alluded to differences in the nature and type of work, his basic position was that work was a loathed activity that workers would naturally aim to avoid.[15] The costs of work were taken as given, rather than as something to be explained.

To be sure, Smith recognized that there were some specific costs linked to the nature of work. In particular, he focused on the costs associated with the division of labour. By allocating separate work tasks to workers, productivity would be raised significantly, adding to economic growth, and with it, wages. Smith gave the example of pin-making to show how workers could produce more output per hour by operating a division of labour among themselves. At a general level, productivity gains would create the basis for a flourishing economy – one where everyone would be able to improve their living standards. But, as Smith stressed, individual workers would suffer a loss in intelligence from the division of labour. Workers who performed the same task over and over again were bound to become 'stupid

and ignorant'.[16] This human cost of the division of labour
had to be weighed against its economic benefit in the form
of higher economic growth and higher wages.

But here Smith's criticisms of work were limited and
ultimately ineffective. Firstly, while Smith acknowledged
the degradation of workers in production, he failed to offer
any solution to it.. All he could offer workers was some
years of basic education before entering the workplace.
Education offered 'homeopathy' for workers – it neither
reduced the burden of work, nor offered the possibility for
better work beyond the division of labour.[17] Rather, the
prospect was of workers losing their intelligence once they
entered work.

Secondly, Smith believed that the stultification suffered
by workers in work was a price worth paying. Extensions
in the division of labour would add to economic growth
and push up wages. The benefits of higher wages, therefore, were put ahead of the disadvantages of work itself.
Indeed, workers were asked to accept the destruction of
their minds, in return for higher wages.

Thirdly, Smith assumed that the pain attached to work
would outlast the reform of work. Because work was
by its very nature a bad thing, it appeared that workers
would suffer work as a pain, even without the division of
labour. Trying to resolve the pain of work seemed futile.
In the end, workers were to accept the hardship of work
as a necessary evil of capitalism. Smith, in this way, set the
foundation for economists and politicians to ignore the
direct costs of work in judgements of well-being.[18]

Later classical economists took the same essential view
of work. Jeremy Bentham, the founder of utilitarianism,
linked work to the experience of negative feelings. He
wrote that: 'In so far as *labour* is taken in its proper sense,
love of labour, is a contradiction in terms.'[19] Bentham saw
the utility of work as arising from its product and never
from work itself. Robert Malthus believed that workers
were lazy and had to be coerced to work. He returned to
the view that necessity had its place in goading workers

into work activity.[20] Malthus's infamous overpopulation thesis added to the view that workers visited harm on themselves (by breeding without constraint) and that punishment (including through the activity of work) was an inevitable part of the human condition. Again, there was no hope for positive change in the nature of work.

The classical economist and liberal philosopher J. S. Mill, took a somewhat different approach. Following other classical economists, he admitted that work was a pain. Writing in 1850, he stated directly: 'Work, I imagine, is not a good in itself. There is nothing laudable in work for work's sake.'[21] Here he agreed with the idea that work was driven merely by the need for income. Yet he also paid close attention to the costs of industrialization. Workers' lives at work were getting worse rather than better through the progress of industry. Mill showed how – far from being an inviolable fact of life – the costs of work were specific to the kind of production and economic system in existence.[22] This more critical angle, as I show below, was given greater clarity and force by Karl Marx and William Morris.

The evolution and consolidation of neoclassical economics from the late nineteenth century to the present have not advanced the economics of work to any great extent. Admittedly, economics has come to redefine the source of the costs of work. Thus, rather than see work itself as a bad, economists have embraced the idea that work is resisted because leisure time is a good. The assumed desire that people possess for leisure time is used to explain why they demand payment for spending time at work.[23]

Still, economic textbooks continue to depict humans as essentially work avoiders. 'Economic man' – the mythical person presented in mainstream economics – is viewed not as a maker or creator, but rather as a compulsive leisure-seeker. The idea is that people will aim to work as little as possible and will only consent to work if their wage demands are met. Work is seen as a merely functional activity that people perform in order to meet their consumption wants. The ideal human state, in turn, is equated with a state of opulent leisure, where consumption is maximized and work is minimized.

The key problem with the standard economics approach to work, as found in all economics textbooks, is that it ignores the effects of work itself on people's well-being. Work is defined as a cost only in a relative sense. The approach neither considers how workers may resist work because of its content, nor attends to the way in which they might embrace work for non-monetary reasons. Instead, the assumption is made that workers are motivated by a desire for leisure and money to spend on goods and services. The wider significance of work – as a constraint on, and enabler of, well-being – is simply ignored.

Modern 'agency theory' – a branch of economics now taught in many business schools – adopts a different view of work resistance: one that recognizes how workers may resist the actual expenditure of effort.[24] The theory assumes that workers have discretion in the workplace and that they will be motivated to use their discretion to minimize effort. 'Shirking' is used explicitly to describe workers' behaviour at work. It is assumed that they must be coerced to work by financial incentives and effective threats of dismissal. Students taught agency theory on MBA programmes are led to believe that workers cause problems for managers (not the other way around) and that workers' shirking behaviour is the universal and central problem of management.[25]

This way of theorizing marks a return to earlier economic thought. In particular, it revives the notion of workers as insufferable idlers found in early mercantilist thought. In effect, it assumes that workers are born to shirk and that they must be forced to expend effort at work. The influence of the environment on workers' behaviour is ignored and there is no attempt to contemplate ways to change work motives by reform. Agency theory, in short, justifies hierarchy and forms of centralized control – indeed, at worst, like mercantilism, it supports managers in actively subordinating workers and perpetuating unequal outcomes at work.

The point to emphasize is that, from ancient times through to the present, there has been a persistent belief that work is something workers are desperate to avoid. This belief has been explained in different ways. One view sees human nature as opposed to work. This view has not always been applied consistently – hence, early mercantilist writers saw workers as prone to idleness, while suggesting that they themselves and other members of the upper classes were ambitious and industrious. Modern agency theory has repeated the same bias by casting workers as 'shirkers', while presenting managers as assiduous in combatting shirking behaviour at work. Class prejudices, therefore, have not been entirely absent from the depiction of work aversion.

A second view has seen work itself as painful. Classical economics painted work as irksome, but did so in a way that obscured and denied the specific causes of the costs of work. A third and final view has presented work as bad because of the assumed delights of leisure hours. This view, as represented by modern neoclassical economics, leaves the direct costs of work undefined and leads to the argument that work can be organized in any form, without harm to workers. This focus on the 'love of leisure' as the reason for workers' resistance to work obscures how work itself can impair well-being, and how change in the organization of work is important in promoting conditions that allow for more rewarding work.

Of course, the above discussion is not meant to deny that work has been, and remains, a source of pain. As numerous studies have shown, there are many instances where work lacks meaning and is experienced as a curse.[26] But these instances do not reflect on anything intrinsic to work, human nature or leisure. Rather, they reflect on how work is organized and structured in society.

The point is that any 'work as bad' thesis fails to the extent that it abstracts from the context and environment in which work is situated. In short, we cannot understand work while we see it merely and exclusively as a cost to be avoided.

The virtue of work

There have also been attempts – again through time – to present the meaning of work in a positive light. These have drawn on different ideological positions and have had different social and political implications. Their effect, invariably, has been to condone work, even while the latter has injured workers' health and well-being. Indeed, ironically, the veneration of work has often impeded moves to realize the benefits of work itself.

The most obvious eulogy to work is the Protestant work ethic that arose in the sixteenth century within Western countries. The origins and influence of this ethic were set forth by Max Weber in his seminal 1905 book, *The Protestant Ethic and the Spirit of Capitalism*. In brief, Weber explained how the rise of Protestant thought – particularly the writings of Martin Luther and John Calvin – helped to establish a set of values in support of hard work. Rather than present work as a means only, Luther and Calvin established it as a sacred activity. By devoting themselves to work, workers could show their faith in God and help to secure their place in heaven. The notion of predestination was used by Calvin, in particular, to convey the idea that hard work on Earth was a key characteristic of those who achieved a position among the elect. Working hard, in whatever occupation, then, could be seen as Godly and a sign of salvation. Workers were called to work by God and work itself constituted a 'calling' that workers had to fulfil. The idea of work as a punishment was challenged and replaced with a view of work as a blessed and spiritual undertaking.

The important point is that the Protestant work ethic developed at a time when work was transitioning towards wage-labour. Prior to capitalism, workers had developed norms and customs that incorporated irregular patterns of working – work was dictated more by the seasons and the weather than by the discipline of the clock, and frequent days off from work were normal (e.g. the weekend was extended by a day, via celebration of 'St. Monday').[27] These norms and customs were ill-suited to capitalism and had to be overcome in order for wage-labour to spread. What the Protestant work ethic did, according to Weber, was provide a means to change attitudes to work. In particular, it offered a basis for consent to continuous working and a regular pattern of work attendance.

As we saw above, mercantilism also sought to change workers' habits by backing the maintenance of poverty. Workers had to be coerced to work on a regular basis and denied the ability to earn more. But this strategy clearly had its limits – indeed, it risked creating resistance and disillusionment amongst workers. In some ways, the mercantilists recognized this fact, by invoking a spirit of nationalism to win support for longer work hours on low pay. They also stressed the virtues of work – hence, by working hard, workers could avoid vices of various kinds. But, on their own, these arguments remained limited. This is where the Protestant work ethic came in. It offered further ideological support for changed work habits. More directly, it channelled religion towards the acceptance of wage-labour, not only as a means to income, but also as an end in itself.

Importantly, the Protestant work ethic did not give positive meaning to work as such, but rather created a justification for workers to work for reasons beyond money. Work might continue to be experienced as a pain. It might also rob workers of their own time and time with their families. It might even injure workers and cut short their lives. But these costs were to be set aside, at least by workers. What mattered was that workers devoted their lives to work, because by working hard on Earth, they could achieve a good life beyond the grave.

This feature of the Protestant work ethic meant that it was always prone to criticism and challenge. The risk was that the erosion of religious belief would lead to a questioning of work and a decline in the work ethic. But the Protestant work ethic served a wider role, by normalizing the pursuit of work for wages. As workers were led to see work as a duty and a basis for elevation, they came to accept the routine of earning and spending money. While initially built on religion, the work ethic became secularized – that is, it acted to win support for the constant pursuit of work. As Weber stressed, even while societies moved away from religion, a devotion to work had come to persist and had enabled the system of wage-labour to reproduce itself.[28] The fact that the work ethic had endured without the direct support of religion showed how the culture of capitalism could recreate itself in ways that were suited to its own expansion.

Beyond Weber, other writers have sought to focus directly on the benefits of work – in some cases, seeking to create their own ethic of work. The nineteenth-century social critic and author Thomas Carlyle, for example, stressed how work was righteous and a source of enlightenment.[29] Carlyle took the view that all work was good, even if it was performed by slaves. Indeed, he opposed the abolition of slavery because he believed that it would deprive slaves of the ability to enjoy the intrinsic rewards of work.[30] If slaves were to become wage-labourers, they would not be guaranteed work – to the contrary, they would face a potentially nomadic existence searching for work. His preferred state was one of strict hierarchy where those at the top of society ruled over the majority, including, it seems, via the continuation of the institution of slavery.

Such sentiments not only lacked humanity but also were flat wrong. Slaves did not enjoy their work, but rather suffered it as an indignity and burden. There was no goodness in slave labour. Against Carlyle's regressive politics, the point of abolishing slavery was to grant slaves the freedom to live and work as they wished. Capitalism might not guarantee work for workers to do, but it at least gave them the option to quit employment that caused them distress. While Carlyle was critical of the restrictions of wage-labour on workers' ability to enjoy the benefits of work, his criticisms were undermined by a vitriolic defence of strong leadership and class superiority.

Carlyle's ideas were repudiated by J. S. Mill. He rejected the 'Gospel of Work' preached by Carlyle. The latter's invective only served to highlight his own lack of sympathy and compassion for the lives of slaves and his opposition to the kind of social reform required to elevate the quality of life. Carlyle had rightly criticized the conditions of industrial work for their lack of meaning, but this criticism was overshadowed by his attempts to reconcile workers to their lives at work. His positive conception of work blinded him to the need to reduce work time and to create greater freedom from work. Mill supported the ending of slavery because it would enable slaves to live and work more freely. He also supported experimentation in alternative work organization (including in worker-owned firms), arguing that moves to widen democracy in the workplace would help to enhance workers' lives. In opposing Carlyle, Mill promoted a 'Gospel of Leisure' – one that aimed at minimizing work, rather than expanding it.[31] His central argument was that progress in society meant lessening the human dependency on work and rejecting the work ethic.

Other ideologies have also evolved that have supported forced labour of different kinds. The most disturbing example here is the Nazi concentration camps constructed during the Second World War. These camps displayed the slogan 'Work sets you free' ('Arbeit macht frei') over their entrances. The elevation of work in this example was used – despicably – to condone human slaughter on an industrial scale. Beneath the apparent praise for work, there existed a deep contempt for human life. In authoritarian regimes in the past and still today, labour camps have also been instituted in order to 're-educate' citizens in prevailing political opinions. Here the redemptive quality of work has been stressed, in spite of its direct human costs. Defences of work of the above kind, wherever they have existed, have only served to mask the injustices and inequities within work and in wider society.

The activity of work continues to be linked to notions of positive or good character. Work remains a key marker of status and position in society. The doctor gains respect for the work she does, while the cleaner is looked down upon because of the work she does. But beyond occupational differences, work is seen as the right and proper thing for a person to do. The cleaner might not command the same respect as a doctor, but she at least pays her way and does her bit for society. Better to be a low-paid cleaner than to suffer the dishonour and shame of being unemployed.

The belief in the value of work drives agendas for reform, including the withdrawal of welfare benefits. The idea of work as something beneficial (and better than unemployment), more generally, creates pressure at a policy level to get the unemployed into work. The danger with this approach, of course, is that we lose sight of how work might itself be a problem and how moving from unemployment to work might lower well-being rather than improve it, if the work that is undertaken is low-quality.[32]

Finally, there is another, more recent effort to eulogize work. This centres on the link established between work and love, presenting the notion that we should all seek work that we love. More directly, following the words of the late Steve Jobs, we should 'do what we love'.[33] That phrase has been refocused on the individual, leading to the slogan 'do what you love'. This slogan has been claimed as an unofficial mantra for modern work, helping to cultivate a deep attachment to work and creating pressure to work long hours, even for no extra pay.[34]

But like previous eulogies to work, 'do what you love' has clear faults. Firstly, it obscures how work is often a barrier to well-being. Indeed, by encouraging workers to accept lower wages and worse working conditions in return for work they love, it can lead directly to lower-quality work. The rise of unpaid internships (often used to gain access to work in the creative industries) is one notable example where the 'love of work' has been used as an excuse to erode wages in a direct way. Secondly, the mantra itself individualizes work, to the extent that collective struggles for change in work are denied. Yet only by mobilizing – including by joining trade unions – can workers effect positive change in work. The plea to 'do what you love', in short, can become an effective means to disempower workers, leading to greater exploitation in work.

Drawing the different strands of this discussion together, it is evident that notions of work as good have persisted through time. These notions have drawn support from competing sources, but they have all had the same impact in terms of justifying and prolonging work. What they have sought to do, more pertinently, is condone work, despite its costs. The irony is that work has been praised universally while its specific costs to workers have endured. It is clear that, by seeing work as all good, we lose the ability to see how work is imposed on workers and how progress is needed to ensure that the work done in society is improved upon, beyond the limits of its past and present forms.

Work and alienation

From ideas that view work as either all negative or all positive, I now address ideas that seek to contextualize work's costs and benefits, not least by making connections to the capitalist system. Marx's contribution stands out here. He combined a deep analysis of work in human life with a powerful critique of work under capitalism. His concept of alienation, in particular, carried weight and significance in his description of the damage inflicted on workers by wage-labour. But, as I will show below, Marx also retained an optimism that work could be transformed from an alienating activity under capitalist social relations into a source of creativity beyond capitalism.

A good entry point into Marx's understanding of work is his critical response to Adam Smith's negative conception of work. As discussed above, Smith took the view, in line with other classical economists, that work would be resisted by people and that the preferred human state was one of unlimited leisure. In the *Grundrisse*, Marx responded directly to Smith, arguing that he had misunderstood the nature and significance of work:

> It seems quite far from Smith's mind that the individual, 'in his normal state of health, strength, activity, skill, facility', also needs a normal portion of work, and of the suspension of tranquillity. Certainly, labour obtains its measure from the outside, through the aim to be attained and the obstacles to be overcome in attaining it. But Smith has no inkling whatever that this overcoming of obstacles is in itself a liberating activity – and that, further, the external aims become stripped of the semblance of merely external natural urgencies, and become posited as aims which the individual himself posits – hence as self-realisation, objectification of the subject, hence real freedom, whose action is, precisely, labour.[35]

Here Marx stressed that work was more than just a way to produce things that humans needed to live – rather, it was also an activity with real importance for the lives of humans as producers. Unlike Smith, who felt it was 'normal' for people to avoid work, Marx highlighted the reasons why people would want to work. In this respect, he admitted that work was motivated by goals external to itself, but he stressed at the same time how the 'overcoming of obstacles' as a part of work could be experienced as a potentially 'liberating activity'. Indeed, Marx suggested that work could become so absorbing and interesting that it could be pursued for its own sake, rather than just for the sake of its 'external aims'. In work, people could achieve 'self-realisation' and 'real freedom'. Far from being an inherent disutility, work could bring purpose and meaning to people's lives.

In taking this position, Marx adopted a distinctive view of human nature. Humans were not natural idlers (as the classical economists asserted) – rather, they were creative beings who would be drawn to productive activity for its own ends. Work, in essence, was part of the 'species-being' of mankind. In his early writings, contained in the *Economic and Philosophical Manuscripts*, Marx stated clearly that 'the productive life is the life of the species. It is life-engendering life. The whole character of a species – its species-character – is contained in the character of its life activity; and free, conscious activity is man's species-character'.[36] Work, for Marx, meant more than just an instrumental activity pursued for extrinsic goals. It also represented 'free, conscious activity'. Humans had innate creative powers and they would look to work as a way to realize these powers. Indeed, through work, they would come to express and affirm their very humanity.

But, as Marx stressed, while work was essential to human life, it had become a source of torment under capitalism. Workers lacked the ability to find meaning in work because of the way that it was structured under capitalism. Rather than work helping to realize their 'species-being', workers endured it in capitalist society as a form of hardship and pain.

Marx used the idea of alienation to describe the costs of work under capitalism. The fundamental problem of work in capitalist society was that it deprived workers of their freedom. Work was not chosen by workers – rather, it was imposed on them by the need to earn wages. In working for a living, workers surrendered the ability to exercise control over the labour process – instead, what they did at work, how they worked and how long they worked were determined by capitalist employers. To be sure, workers could (and should) resist the wages and conditions imposed on them, but they would always resist from a position of weakness that meant that their demands had little chance of being realized. In reality, they faced the prospect of their work being restricted in both monetary and qualitative terms.

Wage-labour, in Marx's view, was a process carried out for the benefit of capitalist employers and to the detriment of workers. While producing 'wonderful things for the rich', waged work produced only 'privation', 'deformity', 'stupidity' and 'cretinism' for workers.[37] Unlike the classical economists, Marx did not universalize the costs of work, but rather saw them as specific products of capitalism. Workers' alienation from work did not constitute an inevitable by-product of the division of labour (as Adam Smith had implied), but rather was a symptom of a system that favoured profit-making over workers' well-being. It was no surprise to Marx that workers shunned work 'like the plague'[38] – rather, this response simply reflected how capitalism degraded work and the worker.

Marx added to his analysis of alienation a theory of exploitation. Workers were assumed to create the basis for profitable production by performing unpaid labour time (or 'surplus value') in work. The focus of tension in the workplace and the ongoing struggle between capital and labour then turned on how surplus value was secured and increased within production. The stress on exploitation added to the view that capitalism was inimical to workers' interests.

Marx made other important contributions, including on the nature and limits of technology. He showed how technology – in principle, a mechanism for reducing work time – had become under capitalism a means to extend the alienation and exploitation of workers. He highlighted how work hours had been lengthened, in spite of technological progress. Indeed, the constant drive to accumulate capital meant there was a tendency for more people to be drawn into work and for the extent and intensity of work to be increased. Machinery itself had been turned into 'an instrument of torture', as opposed to a means for lightening work.[39] As Marx wrote, within capitalist production, 'the machine does not free the worker from work, but rather deprives the work itself of all content'.[40] Under the influence of the profit imperative, work would be deskilled and impaired in quality, intensifying workers' hostility to it. Again, this hostility was not natural or constant, but rather reflected how capitalism undermined the qualitative experience of work.

Three key points can be stressed here in relation to Marx's understanding of work. Firstly, he recognized the positive meaning of work, stressing how, as humans, we have a need for work. He indicated how work was (or could be) purposive and creative. A view of humans as productive beings replaced the classical economists' notion of them as congenital sloths.

Secondly, Marx stressed that work could not be realized as a positive and meaningful activity under capitalism. Objectively, capitalism lacked the capacity to create conditions for human flourishing in work. Indeed, capitalism produced forms of work that made workers feel and act as less than human.

Thirdly, Marx's critique of work led him to contemplate the scope for a new society in which work would be redefined – and experienced differently – as a free, creative activity. This society, in his terms, would be founded on the principles of common ownership and democracy at work. Marx's radical call for change, in short, was based on the idea of making work itself into a source of meaning rather than a cause of alienation. There was hope for better work in the future, provided society ditched capitalism.

Marx believed that capitalism would founder under its own internal contradictions and that socialism would replace capitalism as night follows day. Alienation, therefore, would be abolished in the end. Change would be brought about by a revolution led by the working class, and in the transition to socialism, ownership of the means of production would transfer to workers, allowing for more democratic conditions in which work and life could be reimagined and elevated to a new, higher standard.

Evidently, there are problems with Marx's account. His faith in the idea of a revolutionary working class rising up and overcoming capitalism can be seen as misplaced. He underestimated the capacity of capitalism to create conditions that would sustain consent to wage-labour.[41] Further, his views on the nature of change lacked detail – as we will see below, while Marx set out a grand vision of a future beyond capitalism, he left the facts of how work would be organized in a post-capitalist future somewhat vague.

But there is clear insight to draw from Marx. His focus on the objective limits to meaningful work carries force, as does his emphasis on the need to challenge the way that work is organized. In particular, he challenges us to develop a vision of a better future of work – one that breaks with the present and offers the possibility for work that meets our creative needs. I will consider Marx's own vision of a better future below. In the next section, however, I address the ideas of William Morris on work, largely because they complement those of Marx.

Work as art

As an artist and social reformer, Morris brought a unique perspective to the analysis of work. He recognized that work was neither all bad nor all good. He took from the writings of John Ruskin a positive view of work as art. He stressed how work could be a means for people to gain pleasure in life and showed how the pursuit of pleasurable work should be a goal of society. As he wrote, art was simply 'the expression by man of his pleasure in labour'.[42] Yet, at the same time, he saw how work and art were disconnected under capitalism and how radical reform would be required to transform work. Like Marx, he came to lament the alienation associated with wage-labour and became a convert to the cause of socialism, arguing that the latter was the only way to reconnect work with art.

Morris noted how, in modern society, there was a tendency to see work as good in itself. The morality of work was promoted in a way that encouraged an acceptance of toil. But, in truth, this way of seeing work reflected a dominant ideology – more directly, it reflected the interests of the capitalist class, who profited from the work of workers.[43] Morris intended to expose the real meaning of work under capitalism, namely its existence as a curse-like activity that undermined human well-being.

Morris had several concerns about the kind of work that existed in capitalist society. Firstly, work took up too much time. There was scant opportunity for workers to relax and seek time away from work because they were forced to work around the clock. The thwarting of rest, then, was a key criticism of work under capitalism.[44] Secondly, the capitalist drive for profitability expanded work, regardless of its benefit to society. Here Morris reflected critically on the goals of work under capitalism. The overriding objective of capitalist production was not to create the things that society needed, but to generate higher profits for capitalists.[45] This bias led to waste in production as well as in consumption. Jobs existed that society did not need and that meant little or nothing to the workers performing them, while shoddy and inferior products were created that added nothing substantive to the quality of life. Indeed, it would be better for society if current levels of production and consumption were curtailed and resources were reallocated to different and more valuable ends.[46] Thirdly, there was the lack of pleasure in work, with workers subject to work that was not just pointless, but also painful in itself. Morris stressed with Marx the alienation suffered by workers in work and linked this alienation to a life of unhappiness.[47] Fourthly, there were the external impacts of work on society and on the natural environment. Long hours of unskilled and degrading work produced bad architecture and bad art. They also led to more polluted cities and the destruction of the countryside. For Morris, the waste arising from capitalism was to be

measured by ecological unsustainability and by the reduction in people's ability to live healthy lives.[48]

'Useless toil', as Morris put it, characterized work
under capitalism. Its alien form was reflected in workers'
opposition to work and the destructive force of work on
the economy and ecology. He stressed how technological
progress would only add to the regressive forces evident
in society and would lead workers to suffer even worse
working and life conditions. Morris, like Ruskin, looked
back in time to the era of craft and workmanship that
characterized the medieval period – artisans in the past had
the time and freedom to develop their skills and to produce
great work. Modern techniques, by contrast, had created
not great churches and palaces, but dark satanic mills and
factories.[49] The result was impoverishment, not just of
living standards, but also of work and life. In Morris's
view, while capitalism remained in place, economic, social
and ecological problems were bound to multiply.

Morris's own thoughts evolved over time. From being
a follower of Ruskin, he came to embrace the socialist
thought of Marx. This transition was influenced by his
reading of volume 1 of Marx's *Capital* in 1883.[50] Morris
took from Marx an understanding of the system-wide limits
on human progress – and more directly, on the quality of
work. He emphasized with Marx how capitalism imposed
work on workers and how the expansion of the economy
relied on the continued extraction of surplus value from
workers in work. He also adopted Marx's view on the
inevitability of crisis under capitalism and believed – again
with Marx – that capitalism would give way to socialism.[51]

For the purposes of this chapter, it can be stressed how
Morris saw work not simply as a way to meet material
needs, but also as a means for creative expression. Work
should be art, not drudgery. But he emphasized that the
reunification of work and art would require radical change.
He dismissed all attempts at reform within capitalism and
instead gave his support to a whole new system – one built
on the promotion of artful and pleasurable work. As we

shall see below, Morris joined with Marx in envisaging a future where joy in work would coincide with more free time and where the overall quality of life would be improved, not by negating work, but by lightening it.

Work beyond work

But exactly what kind of future did Marx and Morris envisage? I answer this question in this final section, highlighting how the perspectives adopted by both authors stressed the possibility and indeed necessity of the transformation of work. In their view, the meaning of work had to be changed in the future, and such change could only be realized by reform in the goals, duration, ownership and organization of work.

I begin with Marx's vision of the future of society. As noted above, Marx did not fully spell out what he considered as the ideal society of the future. There was no carefully laid-out plan or blueprint for a better future. Rather, the details had to be worked out after capitalism was overcome. This fact has led to some confusion over exactly what Marx had in mind when he envisaged work beyond capitalism. I will refer to some modern interpretations of his vision of the future.

Marx's view on the future of work was sketched out in a much-cited passage in volume 3 of *Capital*. I quote the passage here in full, in part because it has been the subject of some debate and controversy in the Marxist literature:

> The realm of freedom actually begins only where labour which is determined by necessity and mundane considerations ceases; thus in the very nature of things it lies beyond the sphere of actual material production. Just as the savage must wrestle with nature to satisfy his wants, to maintain and reproduce his life, so must civilized man, and he must do so in all forms of society and under all possible modes of production. This realm of natural necessity expands with his development, because his needs do too;

but the productive forces to satisfy these expand at the
same time. Freedom, in this sphere, can only consist in this,
that socialized man, the associated producers, govern the
human metabolism with nature in a rational way, bringing
it under their collective control instead of being dominated
by it as a blind power; accomplishing it with the least
expenditure of energy and in conditions most worthy and
appropriate to their human nature. But this always remains
a realm of necessity. The true realm of freedom, the development of human powers as an end in itself, begins beyond
it, though it can only flourish with this realm of necessity
as its basis. The reduction of the working day is the basic
prerequisite.[52]

There are several things to take from this passage. One
is the distinction made between the 'realm of necessity'
(where necessary work is undertaken) and the 'realm of
freedom' (where people pursue activities freely). Marx
thought that, with the shift to socialism, time spent in
necessary work would decline and that more time would
be afforded for self-determined activities beyond work.
The extension of the 'realm of freedom' – manifest in the
shortening of the working day – would be achieved both
by the harnessing of 'productive forces' and by the curtailment of work to the fulfilment of need. Socialism would,
therefore, promise more free time. But Marx stressed, too,
the scope for changes in the 'realm of necessity' – indeed,
he outlined how 'freedom' could be a part of this realm,
provided certain conditions were met. These conditions
included workers working cooperatively (or as 'associated
producers') and their taking 'collective control' of work.
Marx suggested how changes in ownership, with workers
deciding jointly on what to produce and how to produce
it, would allow work to be transformed into a free activity.
The idea of workers 'accomplishing it [work] with the least
expenditure of energy and in conditions most worthy and
appropriate to their human nature' added to the impression
that work would be elevated in quality. Workers who had
more free time, in particular, would come to relish doing

work, partly because they would be less worn out by it, but also because they would have the prospect of performing work that they liked doing. The goal was not to expand the 'realm of freedom' to the point where necessary work was eliminated, but instead to create a situation where this realm offered freedom and meaning in the same way as the realm of necessity.

This interpretation is supported by the following quote from Marx focusing on the benefits of reducing work time in a future socialist society. These benefits were to be measured not just by the increase in free time, but also by the enhancement in the quality of work. As Marx wrote:

> It is self-evident that if labour-time is reduced to a normal length and, furthermore, labour is no longer performed for someone else, but for myself, and, at the same time, the social contradictions between master and men, etc., being abolished, it acquires a quite different, a free character, it becomes real social labour, and finally the basis of *disposable time* – the *labour* of a man who has also disposable time, must be of a much higher quality than that of the beast of burden.[53]

This shows how Marx wanted to change the social relations of work. Beyond the reduction of work time, there was a need to shift the goals of production, from satisfying the interests of capital owners to meeting the needs of society. There was also a requirement to abolish the divide 'between master and men' and to bring democracy to work. Such changes would allow for a transformation in the form and nature of work. Specifically, Marx referred to work acquiring a 'free character' and being the basis for 'real social labour', where it was performed for need and under democratic conditions. With ample 'disposable time', workers would come to perform work more effectively. The scope for work time reduction would be increased as workers' productivity rose.

Marx's ultimate goal was to negate alienation and to realize a form of work where workers could experience work itself as 'a *free manifestation of life*, hence an *enjoyment of life*'.[54] The vision entailed creating conditions where work could be enjoyed, not hated, and where humans, as producers, could realize their creative passions not just in free time, but also in their daily work. Marx was passionate about recreating work as a meaningful activity, not accepting it as enforced and painful as the classical economists had done.

Marx felt that cooperative and collective conditions of ownership would allow for greater variety in work. Famously, he referred to people in a future socialist society performing 'one thing today and another tomorrow' – rotating between tasks, from hunter and fisherman to herdsman and critic, without ever being defined by any one task.[55] Marx argued against a strict division of labour and implied that workers under socialism would flourish by seeking out different tasks suited to their own abilities. Workers would work according to their needs and would contribute according to their abilities. In this respect, they would perform work in a way that would add to their well-being. The implication was that, without restricting workers to particular tasks, production could be sustained at levels that would meet societal needs.

Morris accepted much of Marx's vision. He indicated how it was important to reduce work time, not in order to maximize free time, but rather to provide some opportunity for rest. However much work was enjoyed by workers, there was a need to encourage other (non-work) activities that could add to the quality of life. Morris also stressed how the work done by workers needed to change. It was important, in particular, that workers perform tasks that were required by society. The goal would be to ensure that work was useful in terms of fulfilling needs that existed in society. The curtailment of 'useless toil' would itself help to reduce work time, but it would also pave the way for more rewarding and pleasurable work. If workers knew they were performing work for society, they would gain more intrinsic reward from its performance. But it was important too that workers had a stake in work, being direct recipients of the surpluses that were created in production. Morris, like Marx, envisaged the move to a form of collective ownership, where class divisions would be removed and surpluses would be shared equitably.[56] These changes would add to the intrinsic rewards of work, thereby strengthening workers' motivation to work.[57]

Morris's ideas on the reform of technology are note-worthy for the stress they placed on the possibilities for enhancing the quality of work, at the same time as reducing work hours. He argued that, rather than reduce work time to zero by the use of technology, the task to be achieved in the future was reducing the pain of work to zero (or as near to zero as possible). Technology was to be used to make work painless, not to eliminate it. That argument featured in Morris's review of Edward Bellamy's 1888 novel, *Looking Backward*. Bellamy had depicted a future utopia where technology would allow for the elimination of work. He looked favourably upon a life without work because he assumed that work was irredeemably irksome. In his novel, Bellamy argued that automation would help to elevate the conditions of life by removing the need for people to suffer work as a pain. Morris challenged Bellamy's account of utopia. In a review of Bellamy's book, Morris wrote that 'I believe that the ideal of the future does not point to the lessening of man's energy by the reduction of labour to a minimum, but rather the reduction of *pain in labour* to a minimum, so small that it ceases to be pain.'[58] Morris wanted to bring joy to work and this goal remained compatible with reducing work time – shorter work hours would mean raising the quality of work that workers performed. In his novel *News from Nowhere* (1890), Morris set out his own fictional account of a better future – one where joyful labour combined with more free time. He used the novel to show how work could be rescued from capitalism and recreated under socialism as a positive undertaking equivalent to activities performed outside of work.

Morris identified other required reforms for a better world of work. These included attempts to share work that was irksome but not yet open to automation. Cooperation between workers meant everyone taking their share of bad work, where such work could not be replaced by technology.[59] Morris suggested that, where necessary work was intrinsically unrewarding, workers might decide collectively not to perform it and sacrifice some output. Here the sacrifice of output would be justified by the protection of the quality of work.[60] Morris, too, favoured a situation where workers could rotate between tasks (like Marx, he was critical of a strict division of labour), and he endorsed reforms aimed at improving the physical environment of the workplace.[61] Work would only be enjoyed by workers if it was performed under wholesome conditions.[62] Morris, as a business owner, knew how important the conditions of work were for worker morale and well-being, and he favoured creating workplaces that enabled workers to flourish in work. Reflecting again his broader vision for change, Morris showed how the reforms he proposed would help to reduce ecological destruction, while enhancing the standard of life.[63]

In summary, both Marx and Morris emphasized how progress in the quality of work could be combined with reducing work time. It was not about choosing between these goals – say, for example, choosing better work over less work – but rather about seeking to realize both goals simultaneously. But here the stress was on overcoming capitalism to achieve a better future. Society, in effect, had to overhaul the present system of work, if the quality of work and life was to be enhanced.

I will end by suggesting that this point about combining less and better work has not been adopted and accepted in some modern critical thought. Rather, it has been outflanked by a different approach – one that aims for less work and that gives little or no consideration to the scope for better work. This is a clear departure from the interpretation of Marx and Morris given above.

I am referring here to perspectives linked to post-work politics. Several recent books, as mentioned in chapter 1, have focused on the need to minimize work in society. Some authors call for 'the refusal of work' or argue for a 'politics against work'.[64] Others promote the idea of a 'world without work'.[65] These books are important and valuable. For example, they help to promote opposition to work as it exists under capitalism and also support the need for the reduction in work time. Yet I would argue that post-work perspectives fail to grasp the full potential of Marx's (and Morris's) analysis. In particular, they neglect the need – as articulated by Marx and supported by Morris – for change in the form of work. Criticism of work, in short, blocks the case for recreating work as an activity that promotes well-being.

To be sure, post-work writers acknowledge that work can be a positive activity. They recognize, too, that Marx and the wider Marxist literature have considered work to be a valuable activity in its own right.[66] But these writers downplay or ignore the scope for improvement in the quality of work. This reflects a desire not to appear supportive of work when it alienates workers. It also appears to reflect a desire to promote freedom from work, as if this is the main or only route to progress in society.[67]

My point is that emphasis on a post-work future stresses one goal at the expense of another. That is, it gives emphasis to reducing work time, while ignoring the goal of achieving meaningful and pleasurable work. Yet here, as the above discussion has shown, Marx – along with Morris – promoted the goal of improving the quality of work alongside the reduction in work time. In other words, they stressed how better work could be combined with less work, at least in a post-capitalist world.

There is a need for a different view of the meaning of work. Post-work contributions imply that work is bad – there is the same pessimism about work's character as in the writings of Adam Smith and other classical economists. There is no hope for progress in work, on the basis that a life with work is always bad. But an alternative view – one consistent with the above discussion – would argue that work can be enhanced in qualitative terms and that the road to human happiness equates to removing the impediments to good or better work.

This argument is not to blunt the critique of work under capitalism, but rather to strengthen it. In addition to striving, with Marx and Morris, for more free time, there is also scope – again in line with the above writers – to achieve work that is not alienating. Freedom from drudgery, in other words, can be combined with freedom to pursue autonomous activities outside of work.[68] Rather than draw a strict dichotomy between work (a bad) and leisure (a good), it is important to see a way to a future where both work and leisure cease to exist as opposites, but rather jointly contribute to a life well lived.[69]

Let me try to draw this discussion to a close. The vision of 'work beyond work' means challenging and ultimately removing the alienation linked to capitalist work. Modern post-work critics rightly challenge this alienation and give powerful support to work time reduction. My argument here has been that Marx and Morris can help to strengthen the case for change, by showing how joy can be restored to work and how life can be enhanced by freeing up time and opportunity to do joyful activity, whether in work or outside of it. This argument, however, implies the need to go beyond post-work politics, at least as currently defined. In the next chapter, I will develop some of the above arguments by focusing on why long work hours have persisted in society, in spite of predictions and hopes of their demise.

3

The (Lost) Dream of Working Less

The work-cash-want circle is the viciousest circle
that ever turned men into fiends.
                    D. H. Lawrence, 'Wages' (1929)

Work more and change the world. This, at least, is the
view of the business owner and billionaire Elon Musk.
In late 2018, Musk proclaimed boldly that 'nobody ever
changed the world on forty hours a week'.[1] In his view,
world-changing activity requires us to work eighty to
ninety hours per week. Musk himself admitted to working
much longer than this. Indeed, he suggested that at peak
times he works in excess of a hundred hours per week.
He added, however, that the 'sustainable' level of work is
eighty to ninety hours per week.

Musk's comments are notable for several reasons.
Firstly, they imply that prevalent working hours are too
short. He suggests that we should all work more than we do
now. In fact, he suggests the need for a significant uplift in
work hours, effectively abolishing the established norm of
a five-day working week. Secondly, Musk seems opposed
to us having a life beyond work. His whole approach, to
the contrary, is to bind us to work, as if our lives would

be better if we worked all hours of the day. Finally, he is sanguine about the costs of long work hours. To be sure, he admits that pain increases exponentially when we work beyond eighty hours per week. He also concedes that working a hundred and twenty hours a week is 'nutty'.[2] But his view is still that working long hours is always better (for us and society). A working week of eighty hours would bring net benefits to us all. In particular, it could lead to breakthroughs in technology that could help to alleviate pressing societal challenges, including those relating to the present climate change emergency.

Musk's views can be dismissed as exceptional and extreme. Surely no one would believe them – or put them into practice? But Musk is an opinion former, having many millions of followers on Twitter. He may be a maverick in the business world, but his opinions have a wider impact. More directly, they represent a normalization of the idea that working hard is beneficial. As views like his percolate into the media, they offer support for a culture of long work hours. Indeed, by linking longer work hours with the realization of key social and environmental goals such as developing sustainable modes of transport and low-carbon energy generation, these views suggest the urgency of extending hours of work beyond current limits. In the end, working more appears our only hope for progress.

In this chapter, I take issue with Musk's proclamations. I suggest that heeding his advice would inflict harm not only on ourselves but also on society and the planet. Musk's views fit with an ideology that condones the dominance of work rather than challenges it. They fail to see a way beyond the present and towards a future where work is lightened. I argue that long hours of work are a barrier to well-being and that the reduction of work time is a necessary step in improving the quality of our lives. *Contra* Musk, progress in society entails us all working less.

I begin by outlining the prospects of achieving less work in society – specifically, I focus on an essay written by the great twentieth-century economist J. M. Keynes. This essay – first published in 1930 – predicted a future of less work.[3] I outline the vision underlying Keynes's essay and show how long hours of work have persisted, despite his prediction. Finally, I examine different reasons why work hours should be shortened in society and why we should aim to realize Keynes's vision.

In the long run, we will all work shorter hours

As we saw in chapter 2, Marx envisaged a future – beyond capitalism – where work time would be reduced. Marx saw in the reduction of work time the basis for a great improvement in human well-being and argued for socialism, in part because of its capacity to reduce work time. This view was echoed by William Morris, who stressed the barriers to work time reduction under capitalism, and the need to promote more free time in a future socialist society.

Here I focus on a further vision of the future of work time. This vision – set forth by Keynes in a 1930 essay – showed how work hours could be curtailed under capitalism. Unlike Marx and Morris, Keynes believed that capitalism could be reformed in ways that would enable work time to fall continuously. Importantly, it was vital that full employment was maintained and that the proceeds of productivity growth were shared between capital and labour. Provided the right reforms were implemented under capitalism, then, shorter work time could be achieved in the long run.

Written at the onset of the Great Depression, Keynes's essay offered hope for the future. Indeed, it suggested that the 'economic problem' (i.e. the problem of human wants exceeding available resources) could be overcome and that future generations could enjoy a situation of abundance. Looking ahead to 2030, Keynes predicted that the working week could be cut to just fifteen hours. Against socialists who were calling for the end of capitalism, Keynes wanted to see capitalism continue, at least under reformed conditions that combatted high unemployment and high inequality.

Keynes's belief was that the move to full employment would help to accelerate the investment and productivity growth required to shorten work time. By following their instinct for money-making, capitalist employers would make the investments needed to increase productivity. The gains from productivity, in turn, could be used to grant workers both higher wages and shorter work hours. Maintaining full employment would also strengthen workers' bargaining position. For Keynes, reflecting on past trends, workers would favour shorter work hours and would continually press capitalist employers to use the proceeds of productivity growth to reduce work hours.[4] His prediction of falling work hours implied that, with the support of full employment, workers could achieve this reduction.

Keynes assumed certain things about the nature of work and leisure. Firstly, he assumed that work was a painful activity. Like most other economists (see chapter 2), he assumed that humans were averse to work and that happiness would be improved by cutting work hours. He acknowledged that workers had an attachment to work, based on prevailing norms and culture. He referred directly to 'the old Adam' in human nature that drove many in society to keep working.[5] But he believed that human life would be better without work than with it. Progress could not be achieved until humanity was set free from work. Keynes predicted that any work ethic that existed in society would reduce over time and that people would come to embrace and value a life of leisure.

Secondly, Keynes assumed that leisure was good. But here he offered a more active view of leisure than the one found in economics. Leisure did not mean people spending their time idly, but rather entailed their pursuing creative activities beyond work. Keynes felt that people would come to use their freedom from work to realize their talents in activities of their own choosing. In the process, they would gain the ability to enjoy life more.

Keynes did not underestimate the challenges faced by society in adapting to a future of more leisure. People had become so used to working that the prospect of working less could be scary. Keynes noted the example of middle-class housewives who suffered nervous breakdowns through the lack of work.[6] The fear of not knowing how to spend leisure time could impede well-being and even cause mental ill-health. But Keynes was confident that, with time and the right social development, people could find good uses for their leisure time and that the release from work could help to raise the quality of life. Any fear of leisure could be overcome in the future.

Near the end of his 1930 essay, Keynes described in vivid terms his vision of the ideal society of the future:

> I see us free, therefore, to return to some of the most sure and certain principles of religion and traditional virtue – that avarice is a vice, that the exaction of usury is a misdemeanour, and the love of money is detestable, that those walk most truly in the paths of virtue and sane wisdom who take least thought for the morrow. We shall once more value ends above means and prefer the good to the useful. We shall honour those who can teach us how to pluck the hour and the day virtuously and well, the delightful people who are capable of taking direct enjoyment in things, the lilies of the field who toil not, neither do they spin.[7]

The focus on religion, with the reference to a passage from the Bible, signalled the profundity of the change that Keynes contemplated.[8] In all aspects, he envisaged a future where life would be transformed and where the possibilities for living well would be expanded.

Keynes may have written elsewhere the gloomy words 'in the long run we are all dead'.[9] But in his 1930 essay, he signalled how the long run could bring benefit to all. His key message was that capitalism needed to maintain full employment and curb inequality. A reformed capitalism, in short, could deliver a future of abundant leisure.

Two years after Keynes's essay was published, the philosopher Bertrand Russell published an essay called 'In Praise of Idleness'.[10] Russell's essay contained no reference to Keynes's, but the contents overlapped. In particular, Russell's essay argued that society should strive to work less. Russell dismissed the idea that work had any benefit at all and instead focused on the virtues of a life without work.[11] He was concerned that technology was not leading to reduced work hours and that society was faced with the prospect of working the same or even longer hours in the future. This prompted him to call for a radical change in technology's use in society.

The problems of the 1930s – mass unemployment and economic stagnation – overshadowed Keynes's and Russell's essays. The urgent goal was to revive the economy and restore work for people to do. In some cases, this led to consideration of work time reduction. In the US, for example, a proposal for a thirty-hour working week was approved in the Senate in 1933 – however, after remaining in the House of Representatives for five years, it failed to become law.[12] The opposition of industry proved an insurmountable obstacle to reform. But, in general, economic policy was directed at creating work, rather than reducing it. While Keynes had an important impact on the policy debate, his influence was centred on policies that would ensure the return to full employment. Any sense that he had embraced the longer-term goal of reducing work hours was extinguished.

In the post-war period, Keynes's name was invoked to support policies that aimed to sustain high levels of employment. The pursuit of work took precedence over any move to curtail work time – from a policy perspective, more jobs were the priority, not reduced work hours. Work hours did fall in Western capitalist economies, but more through the effects of union power than via the direct intervention of policy.[13] There was an underlying fear – not shared by Keynes or Russell – that if workers worked fewer hours, they would face boredom. While Keynes had predicted that people would adapt to working less and achieve a better standard of life, commentators worried about a permanent malaise linked to the expansion of leisure time. Kurt Vonnegut's 1952 novel *Player Piano* depicted a future dystopia where humans were replaced by machines in work. This fictional account of a vapid life without work conveyed well some of the post-war pessimism around the prospects of a future world where work time was reduced.[14]

Yet, as I will show below, these concerns proved unfounded. Since the 1970s, work hours within capitalist economies have plateaued and even shown signs of increase. Instead of dreams of working less, the nightmare of a life of unending work has loomed large in the public consciousness. Assessing Keynes's prophecy of a fifteen-hour work week by 2030, it seems mildly amusing that someone so intelligent could have got things so wrong.

The never-ending story of work

All evaluations of work time are in some ways relative. Judged by the standards of a century and a half ago, average work hours in capitalist economies are now much shorter. It is true that, as capitalism has progressed, work hours have fallen. In the mid-nineteenth century, for example, it was not unusual for workers to work seventy hours per week.[15] Currently, by contrast, the normal working week for full-time workers in capitalist economies is around forty hours, and in a few countries (e.g. the Netherlands and Germany), it is less. In these countries, shorter working weeks are matched by longer hours of vacation time (see below). Progress in work time from the nineteenth century to the present has entailed increases in paid time off from work.

But we need to add two important points here. Firstly, viewed in historical terms, capitalism has embedded longer hours of work. In pre-capitalist times, work did not occupy the same length of time. While our forebears may not have lived as long as us, they still faced less time at work. The myth is that we have never worked fewer hours, when in reality we work longer than we did before capitalism.[16]

Secondly, as already highlighted, the trend towards shorter work hours has stalled in the last four decades. In some countries, notably the US, work hours have actually increased. The hope of shorter work hours has persisted, but this hope has faced the reality of capitalist economies where work hours have remained stubbornly high.

Table 1 compares average weekly work hours for full-time workers in 1983 and 2019 for selected OECD countries.[17] The table shows the lack of movement in the length of the working week for full-time workers in these countries over the last few decades. Average weekly hours of work lengthened in the US. The Netherlands experienced the largest decrease in work hours, but even so, the standard five-day working week has persisted. The average Dutch worker in full-time employment can still only dream of a four-day working week. In the European context, full-time workers in the UK continue to work some of the longest hours (in the EU, only Greece and Austria have longer hours of work per week).[18]

Headline measures of the length of the working week conceal differences between individuals and groups. For example, managers and professionals work longer hours – work hours, in general, tend to vary positively with income

Table 1 Average usual weekly hours worked, full-time employment, 1983 and 2019 (OECD)

Country	1983	2019
USA	40.9	41.5
UK	42.3	41.5
France	40.2	39
Germany	41.1	39.4
Netherlands	40.7	37.3

(the rich are now more a 'busy class' than a 'leisure class').[19] The self-employed are more likely to work longer hours than those in regular employment, and male workers tend to spend longer hours in paid work than women workers (though, as I will show below, this gap is more than made up by women performing longer hours of unpaid work).

As well, these data capture measured or 'official' hours of work and do not take into account the work done during commutes and at home. New technology (e.g. laptops and smartphones coupled with email) has meant that work has become more a part of commute time as well as home life, adding to total hours of work.[20] This suggests that recorded hours of work are likely to underestimate the actual hours devoted to paid work by workers.

Table 2 shows the trend in annual hours of work from 1983 to 2019. Japan – a country with a culture of long work hours – is added to widen the pool. Annual hours include paid holidays and offer a more extensive measure of hours worked. The table shows that, in all countries, annual work hours fell over the period, though the rate of decline varied between countries. The US and the UK recorded the smallest declines. In France, Germany and Japan, the decline was more pronounced, though Japan's annual hours of work remain higher than in many European countries. The US had the highest annual hours worked at the end of the period.

Table 2 Annual hours actually worked by workers, inclusive of full-time and part-time, 1983 and 2019 (OECD)

Country	1983	2019	% change
USA	1822	1777	–2.47
UK	1568	1537	–1.98
France	1696	1511	–10.91
Germany	1554*	1383	–11.00
Netherlands	1527	1440	–5.70
Japan	2095	1644	–21.53

* This is the figure for 1991. There are no comparable data for Germany in 1983.

The reported differences in annual work hours indicate the importance of the institutional and policy settings in individual countries. In particular, they point to the significance of paid holiday entitlement in allowing for shorter hours of work across the year. The US, for example, has no legal minimum requirement for paid holidays. The result is that one in four American workers do not have a single paid day off.[21] By contrast, all EU countries offer full-time workers at least four weeks of paid holiday.[22] Nonetheless, holiday entitlements have been eroded in the EU since the 2007–8 financial crisis. In Portugal, for example, four national holidays were eliminated in 2013.[23] One price of austerity, in this case, was fewer days off from work. Annual hours of work remain a target for policy intervention and can be manipulated by national governments (e.g. via changes in retirement ages) without necessarily disturbing the length of the working week.

One important feature of capitalist economies over recent decades has been the rise of women entering the labour market.[24] This suggests progress, to the extent that women have previously been denied routes into work and ways to earn a living; however, it has increased work time within households as both male and female members have participated in paid work. As a result, in per capita terms, work hours have risen in capitalist economies since the 1970s.[25]

But the rise in female labour market participation has not seen much change in traditional gender roles within households. Rather, these roles have persisted. Women still take on the majority of housework and care-work in households.[26] The outcome is that female workers have faced a 'double shift', taking on hours of paid work as well as the burden of unpaid work in the home. The overall amount of work faced by women has increased as their participation in paid work has risen.[27] It seems that capitalism has involved women in paid work at the expense of their free time.

Finally, work hours have become more polarized. While unemployment has persisted for some, others have faced underemployment, with work hours restricted below levels that they would prefer. This has become a particular problem in the UK and US, with workers constrained in their ability to access full-time work.[28] But in addition to workers who want to work more, there are also many who want to work less.[29] Work time remains poorly allocated across society.

Despite the expectation of Keynes and others that work hours would continue to fall under capitalism, long work hours have remained for many workers. Years of progress in technology have not translated into shorter work hours – to the contrary, this progress has coincided with the persistence of long hours of work. The question is: why? Below, I address this. I firstly confront the role of power relations in blocking shorter work hours. I then focus on how preferences for work and consumption have created barriers to reducing work time under capitalism.

Power matters

In making his prediction of a reduction in work time, Keynes assumed a specific kind of capitalism. In particular, he assumed that capitalist employers would pass on the fruits of productivity growth to workers. The strength of trade unions, coupled with full employment (achieved by government policy), would put workers in a strong position to win shorter work hours. Keynes believed that a progressive capitalism – one built on cooperation and mutual gain – could create the basis for a future leisure society.

Keynes's assumptions had some credibility in the decades that followed the Second World War. Following his lead, national governments did give priority to alleviating unemployment. They also used progressive taxes to reduce inequality. Trade unions, for their part, remained strong and continued to support workers in the pursuit of better outcomes at work. Capitalist employers, too, ensured that investment was undertaken and that productivity grew. These features were key to the so-called 'golden age' of capitalism and facilitated – in line with Keynes's prediction – the decline in work time.[30]

But, as I showed above, the period since the 1970s has seen the trend towards shorter work hours stall. This reflects on how capitalism has changed. In particular, it reflects how the state has abandoned the goal of full employment, sought via legal action to reduce the power of trade unions and cut taxes for higher-income groups. It also highlights reforms at the level of the firm – specifically, firms have come to place maximizing shareholder value over other objectives (including reducing work time). The upshot of these changes has been a widening in inequality between rich and poor in society.

The trend towards higher inequality has been evident, in particular, within the UK and US. But it has also featured in other capitalist economies, reflecting the wider trend away from sharing the gains of productivity growth and towards a more rapacious capitalism, run by and in the interests of finance capital.[31] The post-war consensus of shared prosperity – one that Keynes sought to encourage – has been sacrificed on the altar of a neoliberal system that has benefitted a minority in society.[32]

The rise in inequality implies that many workers have been unable to work less. Indeed, due to falling incomes, many have been required to work more. The fall or stagnation of workers' incomes has meant they need to work more in order to make ends meet. Reduced union power allied with higher unemployment has also prevented workers from putting pressure on firms to cut work hours, while national governments – eager to appease the demands of a more mobile capital – have been reluctant to implement laws to limit work time.[33]

The important point this discussion raises is that power matters. Most workers are not free to choose the hours they work, but rather are required to work the hours set by those who hire them. In mainstream neoclassical economics, the assumption is that workers can make effective choices over the hours they work.[34] This assumption is replicated in libertarian philosophy and is used to resist the regulation of the labour market. Yet, in reality, free choice is illusory. Workers face real constraints on the hours they work. These constraints have been evident in recent decades, as workers have faced working longer or shorter hours than they prefer. With the persistence of these constraints in the present and future, the prospects of working less are remote, at least without significant changes in the balance of power at work and in wider society.[35]

The focus on power helps to highlight how welfare losses can stem from working hours. In practice, workers may be coerced to work long hours and may be restricted to part-time jobs because of the absence of full-time jobs. Workers are at a power disadvantage in the labour market as well as in the workplace and cannot obtain directly the hours they want. If problems of overwork and underemployment are to be addressed effectively, workers will have to gain more power.

Finally, the conditions linked to COVID-19 have added to work hours, not least by blurring the divide between work and home life. The move to homeworking, indeed, has been associated with longer work hours.[36] If unemployment rises beyond the crisis, then there is the prospect of further stagnation as well as polarization in work hours.

The fact remains that workers are too weak, from a bargaining perspective, to work the hours they desire – in particular, they lack the bargaining power to reduce the working week overall. Keynes may have anticipated that the pursuit of full employment and a more equal distribution of income would maintain workers' bargaining power, but in reality, capitalism has evolved regressively, undermining workers' ability to achieve progress in their lives at work. As a result, Keynes's dream of a fifteen-hour working week has been thwarted.

Demanding work

Keynes predicted that workers would demand shorter work hours over continued working and higher consumption. He assumed both that workers had no strong attachment to work and would seek to embrace leisure as productivity rose and their ability to enjoy shorter work hours increased, and that workers had limited consumption wants. Having achieved their 'absolute needs' through work, workers would aim to work fewer hours. Here Keynes discounted the importance of 'relative needs' linked to the 'desire for superiority' and instead suggested that workers would use the extra income gained from work to buy more leisure hours.[37]

These two assumptions can be questioned, however. Firstly, work has remained attractive to many workers. A negative social stigma attached to not working has helped to maintain workers' commitment to work. But work has also continued to present some direct benefits to workers. From socializing in the workplace to using skills, work has maintained a positive status in society. The anticipated weakening of the commitment to work and the evolution of a strong leisure preference that Keynes implied in his essay have simply not materialized.

Still, there is a need for caution here. While work has its attractions, most workers are in no position to set their hours of work as they wish. Rather, they are still required to work hours set by capitalist employers and face compromises over the time they work. The fact that workers may like the work they do does not mean that they are working the hours they desire.[38] Further, where long hours of work are performed, this may reflect peer pressure and strong financial incentives – it need not reflect any deep desire for work.[39] It remains the case that workers are constrained in their choices over the hours they work, and any enduring preference for work – to the extent that it exists – plays only a very indirect and limited role in setting actual hours of work.

Secondly, the desire for consumption in society has remained strong and prevented the move to shorter work hours. Keynes's prediction of satiation has not been realized – rather, 'relative needs' (or more accurately, wants) have multiplied, pushing workers to work more. In short, the growth of consumerism helps to explain why Keynes failed to predict the course of work hours.

Discussion of insatiability focuses on whether it is innate or socially determined.[40] Humans have an inherent desire to achieve novelty and distinction through the fulfilment of different and diverse wants. In effect, humans are never fully satisfied with what they have, but instead strive for more things in order to find satisfaction in life. The search for distinction, in particular, leads to the pursuit of 'positional goods' that enable their holders to stand out from the crowd.[41] As positional goods are scarce and costly to acquire, competition for their possession leads to an enduring need for more money, which, in turn, drives a high work commitment.

But insatiability also links to the consumption culture that has evolved with capitalism. Within capitalist society, status and distinction are associated directly with possessing objects bought in the market. Another influential economist, Thorstein Veblen, argued that capitalism created a culture that encouraged higher consumption instead of greater leisure.[42] People consumed not simply for need, but also to signal their position in society. Indeed, Veblen coined the term 'conspicuous consumption' to describe how individuals buy non-essential goods and services. Veblen's argument showed how long work hours might be sustained simply because people needed more money to maintain their own frivolous, extravagant and ultimately wasteful consumption.

Advertising and marketing by modern capitalist firms underscore and promote the benefits of higher consumption, while forms of commodification (including those linked to privatization programmes) extend the range of market exchange, to the point where money is required to

purchase most goods and services. Inequality also intensi-
fies competition between individuals – with the rich setting
a high standard for consumption and the rest of society
competing, via consumption, to get ahead of one another.
Capitalism creates a constant desire for greater material
possession, and in turn, a strong drive for long hours of
work. As inequality rises, so this desire and drive can be
seen to grow stronger.[43]

Wage increases can accommodate higher consumption
levels, but where wages stagnate or consumer demand runs
ahead of wage growth, pressure for longer hours of work
may be felt. The rich may be sucked into a search for a
good life through higher spending – one that requires them
to keep working long hours. The poorest in society, by
contrast, may aspire to higher consumption, but then be
faced with more work just to survive. In recent decades,
rising inequality has created a foundation for longer work
hours, by increasing status-driven consumption among the
more affluent and squeezing the incomes of the least well-
off. Rising levels of advertising expenditure and constant
product innovation have only added to the pressure to
work more and consolidated long hours of work for all in
capitalist economies.[44]

Keynes clearly underappreciated how capitalism could
sustain high consumption and long work hours and how
the leisure society he so desired could be denied by capitalist development. Veblen was closer to the mark, in
suggesting that consumerist sentiments would continue to
channel people's behaviour towards higher consumption
and longer work hours. But, as I argue below, Keynes's
case for working less still stands, even if its realization
faces severe constraints in the present.

The benefits of working less

The key benefit of work time reduction is that it would
grant people greater freedom to live as they want. Work

remains a necessity. It exists as an activity that people must do. In capitalist society, it is an activity that is forced on people, by dint of their need for income. The quest for shorter work hours is, then, about winning people's freedom to live with a reduced obligation to work. With more time for themselves, people could cultivate better relations with their families and friends. They would also be able to enter into self-determined or autonomous activities that add to their own well-being.

Past depictions of a leisured future have contained this vision of a better world where humanity is released from work. As we saw above, Keynes linked progress in society with the curtailment of work and the move to a society of expanded leisure. Modern post-work writers have reiterated this vision (see chapter 2), arguing that society should aim for less work as a way to improve the quality of life. This defence of work time reduction rests on humanity gaining the freedom to live without work, and is coupled with an argument for seeking a post-capitalist future.[45]

I agree with this vision, to the extent that it promotes a way of living that is not centred solely on work. Having a full and fulfilling life means doing things other than work. Even for those who love their jobs, there is reason to think that their lives would be better if they had time and opportunity to pursue other activities. For those doing drudgery, there is also the direct benefit of acquiring the time to gain a life outside work. But here I add a note of caution. In particular, following the arguments made in chapter 2, I suggest that the reduction of work time should be about extending opportunities for better work and that its realization should elevate people's lives, wherever they spend them.

Keynes universalized the costs of work without seeing their origins under capitalism. He also failed to see how meaning might be restored to work and how the costs of work could be overcome. His vision of the future was ultimately one-sided. He wanted to win workers' freedom from the disutility of work – he failed to see how progress might be made in the quality of work and how conditions might be created that enable workers to work well. In Keynes's vision, a fifteen-hour work week in 2030 would still remain a source of pain and life would begin for workers only where work ended.

Post-work writers stress how capitalism adds to the costs of work, but like Keynes they see these costs as in some sense irresolvable. There is stress on winning freedom for workers to enjoy their lives beyond work, but little mention of how workers might be empowered to enjoy work itself.[46] Again, the visionary thinking is one-sided, with positive experience linked to free time but not to work time. This thinking fails to engage with Marx's and Morris's ideas about the importance of work in forming human character and in offering scope for meaningful activity. It also misses the opportunity to challenge and reinvent the way that work is thought about and experienced.

I highlight two advantages of reducing work time. Firstly, as mentioned above, there is the advantage of more free time – the opportunity for people to find and develop their talents outside work remains essential to their well-being and provides a compelling reason for shortening work hours. Secondly, there is the advantage of striving for work that is enjoyable. The reduction of work time can help to spread opportunity for more people to enjoy work, not face it as a living hell.

This second point fits with the claim of post-work writers about rejecting work, but here the rejection of work entails the rejection of wage-labour. There remains scope to change and enhance the nature of work by going beyond wage-labour and seeking conditions where work fits into life, rather than limits it. The problem of work is not, then, without solution, but rather is potentially solvable by change in the system of work under capitalism. Against post-work politics, there is hope and need for change in work – indeed, it remains possible to move to a situation where the goal of better work is realized at the same time as that of less work. Again, as argued in chapter 2, realizing this possibility connects to Marx's and Morris's original vision, by asserting that the radical transformation of society should entail extending free time, at the same time as securing more rewarding work.

Work time reduction would also allow for the sharing out of work. This would help to tackle problems of unemployment and underemployment that exist at present. If work hours were reduced to a lower average level, then those who work no hours at all and those who work too few hours could work more. To aid the redistribution of work, there would be a need to extend opportunities for education and training in order to allow people to move into and between jobs. Further, reducing work hours to a lower average level would help to combat the problem of overwork. More directly, if the working week could be cut to four days, then society might create a more even allocation of work across the population, without the harms of unemployment, underemployment and excessive work hours.[47] But the move to a four-day work week would also enable more people to enjoy the benefits that accrue from working. It could help to increase the average quality of work, by minimizing exposure to low-quality work and extending opportunities for entry into high-quality work.

Sharing out work would also help to address issues of gender inequality. Women, as we saw above, tend to do most housework and care-work. Part of the case for work time reduction would be to overturn this pattern and to move towards a more gender-balanced allocation of work. Work time reduction by itself would not resolve gender inequality, but by creating time and space for challenging traditional gender roles, it could help to establish new norms and bring some movement towards equality.[48]

Working less, in addition, would have potential health benefits. There is much evidence that long work hours are linked to poor health outcomes. Working long hours can be associated with higher levels of depression, anxiety and coronary heart disease.[49] Long work hours have also been found to impair cognition.[50] In the extreme, they can lead to premature death (in Japan, the word 'karoshi' is used to define death through overwork).[51] Even where workers choose to work more and enjoy the work they do, it would be better for them and society if they worked less. Public health concerns, indeed, may demand curbs on work time.

Finally, there would be benefits to the environment from working less. The pursuit of more work is associated with more production and consumption. In effect, the constant pressure to work and spend adds to pollution and leads to ecological degradation. As we saw in chapter 2, this degradation and its links to capitalism were highlighted and challenged by William Morris. Recent evidence, indeed, suggests that capitalist countries with longer work hours have larger carbon footprints.[52] This seems to reflect the effect of work hours on consumption – pursuing more work fuels higher consumption directly by supporting higher incomes, and indirectly by creating greater time pressure. For example, workers who work longer hours are more likely to demand and purchase 'convenience' food. They may also be more likely to spend longer hours commuting. Cutting work hours, therefore, would help to shift norms away from higher consumption and towards more leisure – in particular, it would help to encourage less carbon-intensive activities, from more home production to shorter commute times.[53] The point of reducing working time would be to encourage lower consumption, so that the natural environment can be protected rather than sacrificed via the fuelling of an endless work-and-spend cycle.

In countries such as Germany and the Netherlands, reductions in work hours have been realized without loss of living standards. There are also some private companies that have operated successfully a four-day working week. These companies show how shorter work hours can be achieved while maintaining current economic goals.[54]

But the real challenge of reduced work time, in the present as it was for Keynes, is to upend the ways of working and living that are taken for granted. The challenge is to rethink life beyond the constant grind of work and instead to achieve a different lifestyle that allows for more free time. Inevitably, this means shifts in power and the move to more democratic conditions where workers are empowered to decide the hours they work. A key lesson from Keynes is that national governments need to restore full employment and reduce inequality, if work hours are to fall.

I discuss issues of reform – including how a four-day work week might be achieved – in chapter 7. For now, I stress that the case for less work remains a compelling one and one in need of collective action. The important question is how we reform the present system of work to realize it. As I show in the next chapter, the argument for reform is only strengthened once we consider the realities of work in modern society.

4

Realities of Work: From Bullshit Jobs to Good Work

Huge swathes of people, in Europe and North America, spend their entire working lives performing tasks they secretly believe do not really need to be performed. The moral and spiritual damage that comes from this situation is profound. It is a scar across our collective soul.

David Graeber,
Bullshit Jobs (2018)

There is a widespread perception that the present circumstances and conditions of work are failing to meet people's needs. At one level, there is criticism of low pay and the lack of opportunity for people to progress materially in work.[1] At a deeper level, there is concern that the work many people do lacks meaning and purpose – it is of poor quality and without social value.[2]

Yet there remains a strong desire to improve work, not to accept it as something meaningless. In particular, there is a quest for work that brings dignity and light to the lives of those performing it. Improvement in the quality of work is linked to creating meaningful work, in which workers value work and gain enjoyment from its performance. This allies with a hope and demand for a future where the costs of work can be overcome and higher-quality work can be extended to the many, not the few.[3]

In this chapter, I consider how the understanding of work's meaning has been captured in some modern commentaries. I begin with the thesis of 'bullshit jobs', devised and popularized by David Graeber.[4] This thesis has gained prominence in recent years – indeed, it has become a key focus for radical criticism of the nature of work in contemporary society. Graeber is dismissive of attempts to praise work – instead, he argues that work is a barrier to well-being. For him, meaningless work exists because it suits the interests of the powerful, and the only hope for progress in society rests with extending people's freedom to live without work. He favours a UBI to create the conditions for a future with less work – one where people's lives are enriched by having time on their hands to do what they want.

I offer criticisms of Graeber's thesis, from an economic and political perspective. I argue that his thesis fails to offer an adequate account of the meaning of work. Indeed, due to its subjective basis, it blunts criticism of work under capitalism and hinders the articulation of the case for change.

I then tackle perspectives that examine the link between work and happiness. Some authors connect work directly to unhappiness, confirming the view that work is a bad. Others, however, claim that work is beneficial, at least relative to unemployment. These competing perspectives, I argue, lack clear insight into the structural constraints on workers' ability to achieve well-being in work, and add little or nothing to a politics aimed at reforming work.

Finally, I consider the quality of work. I argue against subjective definitions of the quality of work based on the use of survey data, and instead make the case for an objective definition that focuses on the nature of jobs that workers actually perform. I argue that an objective definition of the quality of work can help to criticize work in the

present, while aiding progress towards realizing a different
and better kind of work in the future.

Bullshit jobs

At the outset, let me mention that Graeber is not the first
author to challenge the meaning of jobs in society. In an
earlier book, Studs Terkel also reflected on what he saw
as the 'violence' of work that many workers faced in their
jobs. Based on interviews with a wide range of workers,
Terkel showed how people struggled to find fulfilment in
work – instead, they were faced with the 'daily humiliation'
of performing jobs that were too small for their spirits.[5] To
be sure, Terkel acknowledged that some workers sought
to compensate for the distresses of work, by creating their
own distractions and sources of meaning in work. But
their efforts to get through the working day were made
against a background where their interests did not matter
and where jobs were structured by bosses. Work remained
a means to earn a living, more than a way of enjoying
life. Most workers longed for the day when they could be
released from work's restrictions.

Graeber's thesis on bullshit jobs offers a new interpretation of work's 'violence'. The thesis itself was originally
set out in a short blog post for an online magazine. The
blog gained widespread – and indeed global – attention. It
subsequently became the basis for a book-length treatise
on the theory of bullshit jobs.[6]

At the heart of this theory is the idea that a large number
of existing jobs lack meaning, in the sense that they do
not contribute any direct societal value. Rather, these jobs
exist merely to keep people busy and to fill their time. The
argument is that those in power prefer people to be busy
than to have free time, and they have allowed socially useless jobs to persist in order to maintain the existing social
order. While corporations could save costs by liquidating
bullshit jobs, their owners and managers have retained

these jobs as a way to prevent the kind of social upheaval that would occur if free time was extended.

Bullshit jobs include high-paid occupations such as corporate lawyers. They also include the army of administrators that exist in modern organizations. A particular example Graeber gives is the expansion of administrative functions in universities – these functions (including many new jobs) are viewed as essentially useless. In part, they exist to show the power and status of a managerial elite (Graeber refers to 'flunkies' who are employed by managers as signs of their own power and prestige) – in other ways, they exist to keep their incumbents occupied. Graeber describes a process of 'managerial feudalism' with hierarchies created within organizations – both private and public – that feature powerful people generating myriad bullshit jobs to make themselves appear important. Finally, there are the jobs required to furnish the needs of those who hold bullshit jobs, from dog-washers to pizza-delivery drivers. These jobs have driven the growth in the so-called 'gig economy'. Their existence, in this context, is linked to the busyness of a cadre of workers whose gainful employment generates no direct social value.

Graeber contends that workers know when their jobs are pointless and unnecessary. It is evident to workers who perform bullshit jobs that their jobs could safely disappear with no loss to society. Yet they go on consenting to perform them, in part because they need paid work to live, but also because they regard work as the 'right thing' to do. An ethic of work still compels workers to carry out jobs, even while they are known to be pointless. Workers may resent their jobs and complain about being unhappy at work, but they fear disapproval for being without work. They consent to work, despite its pointlessness.

Graeber suggests that the existence of bullshit jobs, though recognized by many in society, is rarely spoken about in public. This is, in part because people do not want to admit publicly they are doing bullshit jobs – rather, they would much prefer, for reasons of status and reputation, to pretend that their jobs are not bullshit. This preference, though, cannot conceal the fact that workers know secretly that they occupy bullshit jobs. Graeber's contribution is to expose as well as critique the phenomenon of bullshit jobs, with a view to promoting a future where their presence is minimized and ideally eliminated.

Direct evidence on the number of bullshit jobs in existence is limited. Instead of data analysis, Graeber points to the results of a 2015 survey conducted in the UK. This survey asked workers the following question: 'does your job make a meaningful contribution to the world?' Of those who responded to the survey, 37 per cent said that their jobs did not make a meaningful contribution (another 13 per cent said they were uncertain, while 50 per cent answered positively).[7] In interpreting this result, Graeber is clear that workers are the best judges of the meaning of their jobs, and if workers say that their jobs make no meaningful contribution to the world, they should be taken at their word. Based on the above data, he claims that half of existing jobs in the UK are bullshit.

Note that Graeber defines bullshit jobs in separation from the content of the jobs themselves. Workers may well enjoy positive working conditions, but still be in bullshit jobs. They may also gain respect through doing their jobs and be recognized for their efforts – indeed, they may have high status in society. The quality of work that workers perform and the recognition they gain from work are beside the point when it comes to classifying bullshit jobs. What matters is the meaning that workers ascribe to the jobs they do – again, if workers say in surveys that their jobs are pointless, then this must be taken as clear evidence that their jobs are bullshit.[8]

That said, there is the strong suggestion throughout Graeber's book that workers dislike performing bullshit jobs (the numerous testimonials of workers corroborate this). For one, workers are doing jobs that they know should not exist. For another, their time at work is mostly spent finding things to do, from updating Facebook profiles to surfing the Internet. The meaninglessness of jobs is reflected in a lack of purpose and satisfaction in work itself. In all respects, workers would prefer to be doing something else with their lives. Bullshit jobs, it is argued, are sites of oppression, rather than sources of fulfilment. Only the need for income and commitment to the work ethic keep workers from leaving.

Graeber sees the proliferation of bullshit jobs as a barrier to the reduction of work time. He returns to Keynes's famous prediction of a fifteen-hour working week by 2030. As we saw in chapter 3, Keynes believed that higher investment and higher productivity would lead to a reduction in work hours. Graeber suggests that Keynes was right, in the sense that progress in productivity has lessened the work required to meet basic needs. Manufacturing, for example, has shed labour. Many of the jobs that Keynes confronted in his day have been eliminated, as productivity in manufacturing has accelerated. The reason for the failure of Keynes's prediction lies not in the lack of productivity to lighten necessary work but in the capacity of the economy to create more bullshit jobs. Against Keynes's prediction, capitalism has continued to generate 'make-work' jobs, preventing the expansion of free time.

Graeber also dismisses arguments that associate the failure of work hours to fall with the rise in consumerism. He argues that many jobs that now exist are not linked directly to consumption – rather, they are associated with administrative and other 'unproductive' functions. The stress on consumerism also misses the politics of work's persistence – namely, that work is needed to prevent the spread of leisure. People's lives are still filled with work, in short, not because of their unyielding desire to buy more things, but because of the political need to ensure that they are not given the opportunity to self-create beyond work. 'The ruling class', as Graeber puts it, 'has figured out that a happy and productive population with free time on their hands is a mortal danger'.[9] This consideration has underpinned resistance to work time reduction and explains why work hours have stayed long in capitalist economies.

On pay, Graeber illustrates how the monetary rewards from work are inversely related to the social value contributed by workers in jobs. Carers, for example, get paid vastly lower wages than corporate lawyers. Yet society could not live without carers, though it could easily get by without corporate lawyers. This argument has had particular resonance in the context of the COVID-19 crisis, where the social value of 'key workers' – and their relatively low pay – has come to be more widely appreciated.

Graeber's thesis offers a damning indictment of the present system. He suggests that jobs exist merely to suit the interests of powerful vested interests. He argues that those in power (i.e. 'the ruling class') have mobilized the idea of work as a morally valuable thing to do in order to justify work's continuation. In all this, workers have suffered. Not only have they been denied the freedom to live as they please; they have also been subject to jobs that they know are meaningless. Workers who perform bullshit jobs face not only a deep sense of inauthenticity, but also potential mental and physical ill-health. The moral and psychological cost of bullshit jobs is seen as high.[10] Graeber sees the presence of bullshit jobs as a sign of the irrationality of the present economic system and as indicating the need to create a different system where work is curtailed and ultimately abolished. Hence, if all the bullshit jobs were extinguished, it would be possible for society to reach the fifteen-hour working week predicted by Keynes. It would also be possible for more people to live healthier and more enriching lives outside of work. Without the constraints of bullshit jobs, in short, life would be more meaningful.

Graeber's book is full of detail on the different types of bullshit jobs (from 'goons' through 'duct tapers' and 'box tickers' to 'taskmasters') and on the negative experiences of undertaking these jobs. He also charts the reasons for their increase, the barriers to their elimination and the interventions required to change society. He argues for a

UBI as an effective mechanism for freeing people from the limitations and burdens of work.

Yet, as provocative as Graeber's book is, there are areas for disagreement and criticism. Firstly, there is more than a hint of conspiracy theory to the thesis of bullshit jobs. The powerful may have reservations about the move to a leisure society, but this does not mean they will persist with inefficiency, especially while the latter erodes profits. Recent history has shown how businesses have downsized and sacked workers in order to lower costs.[11] This goes against the idea of bullshit jobs becoming the norm. There are also ways for firm owners and managers to maintain power without necessarily keeping workers in meaning-less jobs – for example, forms of monitoring and insecure employment contracts have been used to exert control over workers, so there is no need for these owners and managers to artificially create and sustain work for political reasons. Further, if bullshit jobs were so prevalent, there would be low levels of unemployment and underemployment – yet, especially in periods of crisis, the latter have both risen, suggesting again that, beyond the contrivances of the powerful, there are material forces driving the volume and distribution of work in society.[12] These forces, of course, include firms' profitability and state spending on public services. University administrators, for example, are just as vulnerable to austerity policies as care-workers.

Secondly, there is a related neglect of broader shifts in the economy. The last few decades, in particular, have seen power shift towards financial stakeholders.[13] The latter have gained influence at the same time as national govern-ments have retrenched welfare states, liberalized labour and financial markets and reduced the power of trade unions. Importantly, these changes have limited workers' ability to bargain for better pay and improved working conditions – indeed, they have led to declines in the quality of work. For example, the intensity of work has risen.[14] The point here is not that work has suffered some loss of meaning, but that this loss is linked to workers' reduced bargaining power – a process associated with changes and reforms in the political economy of capitalism. Though referring to power relations, Graeber fails to make clear the link between these relations and the capacity for work to change (including in ways that are disadvantageous to workers). Developments and trends in the economy, in general, are eclipsed by a slanted rhetoric that stresses the covert actions of a powerful elite. Indeed, the repeated reference to 'feudalism' blurs the status of capitalism itself, including the profit imperative and the power relationship between capital and labour.

Thirdly, the notion of bullshit jobs is overly subjective. As mentioned above, this notion is linked directly to workers' own assessments of the meaning of their jobs. In the same survey used by Graeber, 50 per cent of UK workers said their jobs had meaning, countering the view that bullshit jobs are all-pervasive. A further 63 per cent said their jobs were very or fairly 'personally fulfilling', implying that workers had a deeper connection to work than just a blind adherence to the work ethic.[15] Workers have mixed feelings about work – indeed, some workers can feel both affinity with, and resentment towards, their jobs, depending on what aspect of work they are focused upon.[16] To paint jobs as entirely bullshit, in short, is to miss the variation in the quality of work across jobs.

Think, for example, how Graeber groups together jobs such as corporate lawyers and pizza-delivery drivers under the same heading of bullshit jobs. The implication is that these jobs are commensurate. Yet on any criteria (e.g. pay, prospects, pensions and status), corporate lawyers can be seen as much better-off than pizza-delivery drivers. Lumping together myriad jobs under the same generic heading loses focus on the specific aspects of work that shape workers' ability to achieve well-being. As a result, criticism of low-quality jobs (such as pizza-delivery drivers) is made less effective.[17]

Fourthly, Graeber's contribution misses the scope for change in work. The stress on the pointlessness of work (defined in subjective terms) suggests that work should be eliminated. Only by not working can people achieve a life of meaning. Admittedly, there is some residual praise in Graeber's book for non-bullshit (or 'real') jobs, though the precise definition of these jobs seems arbitrary – if subjective assessments are all that counts, then there are no objective criteria for choosing between bullshit and non-bullshit jobs, leaving analysis of the meaning of work completely open-ended (see below). But putting this issue to one side, there is an 'anti-work' thesis built into Graeber's approach. In effect, meaning is seen to come from outside of work as opposed to from within it. As a result, there is no link to other critical theories of work, including Marx's, that suggest the opportunity and need to bring meaning to work.

On this last point, Graeber is another example of a post-work critic seeking to dismiss all work, without close regard to the scope for its transformation. There is criticism of wage-labour and the work ethic, but this leads to support for a world with zero work. Missing is the kind of visionary thinking of Marx (together with William Morris) of rebuilding society in ways that encourage better work with more free time. The notion of bullshit jobs, in the end, inhibits understanding of the possibilities for rethinking and recreating work beyond the present.

In summary, the bullshit jobs thesis has evident potency. Politically, it challenges the status of work in modern society and calls for a reimagining of life in the future. Its subversion of work in its present forms is important and timely, as is its insistence on the need to create less work. But, as mentioned above, it also has aspects that can be questioned. The point is that the critique of work needs to be widened beyond the conception of bullshit jobs if it is to tackle and resolve the problems with work in modern society.

The ills of work

Other modern accounts of work stress the negative experience of work itself. These accounts focus less on the meaning of work and more on the direct effects of work on well-being. A recurring theme is that work cannot – at least in its existing forms – create the conditions for people to live happy and healthy lives. To the contrary, work reduces happiness and health.

Alex Bryson and George MacKerron, to take one example, report findings that support the idea that work is a bad.[18] Indeed, they suggest that work is one of the worst activities that people can experience in their lives. The evidence they provide is used to vindicate the view found in mainstream neoclassical economics that work is a disutility (see chapter 2) and that life is better for people where work is absent.

Bryson and MacKerron's study uses a novel survey method, namely an app (called 'Mappiness'), which people can upload on to their smartphones (the app has been collecting data since August 2005 and has tens of thousands of users). Those who sign up to the app are contacted at random points in the day. Once contacted, they are asked to rate their happiness. The benefit of the app is that it provides an 'in the moment' measure of happiness – it does not confront the same biases that arise with standard evaluative questions about subjective well-being. Hence, when people are asked to evaluate their experiences in surveys, their responses are often clouded by particular events that have a significant influence on their well-being. There is also a potential recall problem where the happiness gained from activities is not accurately conveyed. With the Mappiness app, by contrast, there is scope to capture people's well-being at the moment they are undertaking particular activities, including those they perform at work.

Bryson and MacKerron acknowledge that research shows how the employed have greater subjective well-being than the unemployed. It seems that being in work boosts happiness relative to being out of work and that there are benefits in moving from unemployment to employment.[19] Interpreting this research, they argue that the positive effects of work on well-being may reflect the meaning that comes from undertaking paid work. Thus, in a world where participation in paid employment is viewed as 'normal' and where status comes from having a job, performing work may be considered to have some benefit to people's well-being.[20]

Yet, notwithstanding this benefit, work activities have a direct impact on subjective well-being. People may prefer being in work to being unemployed, but this does not indicate how they feel about work during the time they spend at work. This is where the Mappiness app is seen to have value, in gaining an insight into how much happiness people derive from the hours they work.

In their study, Bryson and MacKerron use data gained from Mappiness to estimate the link between happiness and work activities. Their regression analysis focuses on the same individuals over time. What they find is that, out of forty possible response options, time spent at work ranks the second lowest in terms of subjective well-being. Hours of paid work reduce happiness by 7–8 per cent compared with a situation where no work is undertaken. Only being sick in bed ranks higher than paid employment in terms of momentary unhappiness.[21]

The results are sensitive to the kind of work that people undertake. Homeworking, for example, reduces the level of unhappiness associated with paid work. People also tend to report lower feelings of unhappiness where they work with others and with friends. This suggests that policy action (e.g. more homeworking) can be used to boost people's reported happiness.

Bryson and MacKerron, finally, examine whether the result of the negative effect of work on happiness is due to the pressure and stress of work. Yet, after controlling for feelings of relaxation, they find that people still report lower happiness levels while at work. The combination of work with other activities that are pleasurable also fails to remove the unhappiness associated with work. The conclusion is that work is truly something most people want to avoid, unless compensated by wages. Again, this seems to support the view of mainstream neoclassical economists that work is an inherent bad.[22]

Bryson and MacKerron's study is undoubtedly thought-provoking. But it also has some limitations. Firstly, it fails to consider directly the environment of work. The limits of the data mean that the characteristics of work as an influence on workers' well-being are missed. This fact leaves the reasons for the negative association between work and happiness open-ended. Is the problem that work is experienced as painful or is it that work takes time away from leisure? In mainstream neoclassical economics, there are different views on the costs of work, and the test of the disutility of work performed by this study fails to adequately discriminate between these views.[23]

Secondly, the approach taken by Bryson and MacKerron reduces work to the level of a feeling inside workers' heads. It lacks any broader sense of how work may shape workers in ways that go beyond their feelings. The fact that work can be alienating is not considered. There is reference to workers' negative feelings (reported via an app), but nothing on their sense of disillusionment and disempowerment at work. Equally, there is no idea about the potential creative aspects of work and the latter's role in creating space for fulfilment beyond immediate feelings of pain or pleasure. Methodologically and conceptually, the treatment of work as a disutility (or negative subjective feeling) fails to capture the deeper meanings of work.

Thirdly, Bryson and McKerron's research reaches the same conclusion as other negative accounts of work. That is, it resigns us to the cost of work, without much hope of its negation. Following standard economic theory, the study emphasizes finding compensation for work's cost via higher wages and higher consumption. This approach misses the needs that people have for work that brings benefit to their lives. It also overlooks the capacity for interventions that help to enhance the work that people do, such that it presents opportunity for meaningful activity, rather than just prevents episodes of momentary unhappiness.

Jeffrey Pfeffer offers an alternative and more critical interpretation of the distresses of modern work.[24] He focuses directly on the toxic environment in many contemporary organizations. Work has become more demanding as well as more stressful due to the adoption of particular management practices. The rise of the shareholder value model, specifically, has created a results-based and cost-cutting form of management. Under the influence of this, workers have faced job cuts as well as wage freezes. They have also confronted punishing work schedules and long work hours. The effect of modern management practices has been a marked decline in workers' health. Indeed, many workers have died through their exposure to hard and oppressive work environments.

Pfeffer links the burdens of work with excess mortality rates. In one paper, he estimated that an additional 120,000 deaths annually in the US could be attributed to the effects of regressive management practices. The extra health-care costs were estimated at $190bn per annum.[25] While policy-makers are rightly concerned with excess deaths due to smoking and drug use (along with diseases such as dementia and cancer), they should also pay close attention to high mortality rates linked to workplaces.

Here Pfeffer's findings complement those of other studies of the health impacts of work. In the UK, for example, a study of British civil servants found that low levels of job control contributed to poor health outcomes. The risk of having a heart attack was linked directly to not being in control of one's work.[26] Again, there is clear evidence that work can be a direct (and even fatal) health hazard.

Pfeffer argues that poor and life-limiting management practices have become embedded within organizations partly via the influence of theories that preclude alternative ways of managing. Economic theories taught in business schools have promoted the sovereignty of shareholders and the need to pursue short-term profitability, in particular.[27] The dissemination of these theories to managers via MBA programmes, in turn, has cultivated a common sense that management should be pursued in ways that are beneficial to shareholders and that maximize profits (regardless of the costs to workers). And, in a performative way, belief in these theories has created a reality that accords with the theories' predictions. Managers have made 'real' the economic theories taught to them in business schools through acting as if they are true.[28]

'Bad' management practices – linked to the 'bad' economic theories taught in business schools – are obviously harmful to workers, but they also limit organizations' efficiency. Pfeffer argues that the focus on maximizing shareholder value has added to firm costs, through lower employee engagement, higher turnover rates and reduced job performance. While business schools have continued to teach a particular way of managing organizations, the effect of managers following this teaching has been to lower efficiency within organizations. Managers are trapped by a way of thinking that makes bad management the norm.

Instead, Pfeffer proposes a different approach to management – one that is sensitive to workers' needs and that promotes forms of shared prosperity. Stress is placed on promoting 'good' theories of management in business schools and using these as a way to reform management practice. There is also a wider argument that organizations should promote goals of well-being and sustainability. This emphasizes how management that is good for workers can deliver positive outcomes for profit-maximizing firms.

Pfeffer's contribution, unlike that of Bryson and MacKerron, addresses explicitly the effects of the conditions and organization of work on workers' well-being. Unlike Graeber, Pfeffer also sees room for change and reform. He does not dismiss entire jobs as bullshit, but instead uncovers the barriers that prevent workers from gaining a healthy and fulfilling work life. There are ways to improve the quality of work – for example, via moves to increase workers' autonomy.

Yet problems remain in Pfeffer's approach. Firstly, he focuses very much on the ideational level – in particular, reforms are assumed to come from managers acting on different theories and ideas about management. The element of persuasion – of imploring managers to act differently – underestimates the structural constraints on reform. Business schools, for example, may adopt different theories, but little may change in the form of management that exists within organizations. Indeed, bad management may persist, despite what business schools teach and profess. Rather, real change requires shifts in ownership and control.[29]

A second problem concerns the understanding of work itself. The stress on management practices limiting workers' well-being together with organizational efficiency is important and powerful. But it leaves undisclosed the deeper-lying problems of work. Fundamentally, work is problematical because it is imposed on workers and is conducted within the parameters of the wage-labour relation. It is also a problem because the aims of production are based on profitability. Toxic workplaces reflect a system that is not designed to meet workers' interests, but instead is aimed at creating higher returns for capital owners. Pfeffer hints at inequalities of power, but then implies that exhortation and good leadership can make a difference at work, ignoring the deeper reasons for the persistence of bad management, and with it, bad work. Deaths due to work, in short, will not be reduced by calls for managers to change course and to perform management differently.[30]

My point here is that, for all the merits of Pfeffer's approach (and its advantages over alternative approaches such as that of Bryson and MacKerron), it still does not quite grasp the full realities of work as it exists under capitalism. I suggest in the next section that there are other approaches where work is treated as an activity that is, in all cases, beneficial. These approaches create other barriers to reform, and in this respect, must be a focus for criticism.

The costs of unemployment

The idea that work is good has drawn strength from the view that unemployment is bad. Evidence, as mentioned above, suggests that unemployment erodes well-being. Indeed, this evidence suggests that unemployment has long-lasting scarring effects on workers. Many workers find it hard to recover from unemployment and may suffer lower well-being even after re-entering work.[31]

The costs of unemployment include not just the loss of income, but also the loss of status and the loss of opportunity to participate in work. Marie Jahoda studied the non-pecuniary losses from unemployment in the 1930s.[32] Her research revealed how the loss of work directly impaired workers' well-being – indeed, it led to despair and depression. Recent evidence from studies of subjective well-being have confirmed the negative effects of unemployment on people's lives.[33]

Other research has shown how unemployment can lead to reduced years of life. In their 2020 book, Anne Case and Angus Deaton refer to 'deaths of despair'.[34] They show how, in the US, unemployment within particular communities – notably, the white working class – has led to increased alcohol and drug addiction. Without the structure of work and the opportunity to earn a decent living, people have been pushed into types of behaviour that have ultimately cost them their lives. Suicide rates have risen, reflecting the lack of opportunities available to these people. The 'work' aspect is crucial for Case and Deaton. In the past, well-paid, full-time jobs in manufacturing were the glue that held working-class communities together. Now the removal of these jobs and the rise of joblessness has led to social fragmentation and individual despair. The result has been a fall in life expectancy in the US.[35]

The costs of unemployment are clearly significant and signal the need for policies to resolve it. Not all jobs are bullshit and work is not merely a disutility. Indeed, as authors like Jahoda recognized, work can bring some direct benefits to people's lives. But it need not be accepted that just any kind of work should be provided. One problem with some approaches is that they move from highlighting the losses in well-being linked to unemployment to recommending that work be created, almost regardless of its quality.

Richard Layard, for example, argues that unemployed workers should be required to take any available work (including bad work) because that is the best way to raise their happiness levels.[36] He recommends that cash benefits be limited to ensure that unemployed workers find and secure work. Such an argument neglects the fact that work has its direct costs and that a better life for the unemployed may entail improving the quality of available work. In effect, by forcing the unemployed to take low-quality work, policy-makers may end up reducing well-being rather than raising it. Research, indeed, highlights how workers can suffer worse health outcomes by moving from unemployment to poor-quality work.[37] This underlines the fact that well-being depends not simply on being in work, but also on performing work that is high-quality.

While it is true that there are 'deaths of despair' linked to unemployment, there are also arguably 'deaths of despair' linked to low-quality work. Pfeffer's writings are again useful here in showing how low-quality work can be as much a problem as high unemployment, and how there is a need to tackle and remedy the negative health and well-being consequences of work alongside resolving unemployment. It is not about promoting work at any cost, but finding ways to secure work that enhances people's lives. But how exactly should we define the quality of work? This particular question is addressed below.

The quality of work

Definitions of the quality of work come in different forms. Bryson and MacKerron reflect an approach in modern mainstream economics that sees the quality of work as a subjective concept. In effect, workers report their feelings about work through survey instruments and this provides the basis for defining the quality of work. If workers rate work as dissatisfying or painful in a survey, then this is sufficient proof that work is a disutility.[38] Graeber, though coming from a radical perspective, adopts a somewhat similar approach. He uses survey data to establish whether jobs are meaningful or not. These data are seen as a reliable guide for counting the number of bullshit jobs in existence.

But subjective approaches like these present clear problems. Notably, they imply that subjective assessments of the quality of work are unbiased, when, in reality, they are subject to biases of different kinds. Some workers may report their jobs as satisfying and meaningful in surveys because they have low expectations about work – their positive reports about their jobs may simply reflect some kind of satisficing behaviour, where work is judged as 'good enough'. They may report feeling positive about work, despite the fact that the work they do is lacking in key qualitative dimensions (for example, their jobs may be low-paid and offer few intrinsic rewards). Positive reports of the quality of work, then, may conceal the real adversities that some workers face in work.[39]

Take the example of Graeber. Using survey evidence, he finds that many workers report their jobs lack direct meaning. This remains a striking result, but on its own, it means very little. Specifically, the data offer a noisy signal of the quality of work, given that workers' evaluations of the meaning of work can be biased by norms and expectations. Maybe the headline number of bullshit jobs is an underestimate of the extent of meaningless work because it fails to capture how many workers have low expectations about the meaning of work? Perhaps it is an underestimate, too, because it fails to capture how some workers have adapted to the low meaning of their jobs? Reports of meaningful work might then be inflated. From a different perspective, the survey data Graeber uses may also be biased by those in jobs with meaningful features who have decided, due to the influence of high norms and expectations, their jobs are not up to the standard they desire. Here research may conceal how (in the case of corporate lawyers and other high earners) some jobs in society have clear positive attributes.

Graeber, in practice, has some objective criteria for the quality of work. He judges that bullshit jobs are meaningless because they are being imposed on workers and are filling time rather than contributing directly to society. But these criteria remain implicit and are not clearly defined. An objective approach to the quality of work needs to be developed explicitly and applied directly in the assessment of work in reality.

The starting point for an objective approach is that work matters beyond how it makes people feel – instead, there is a focus on the role of human needs and their fulfilment, or not, through work. Needs relate, at a basic level, to the requirement for food and shelter. But they also extend to high-level requirements such as that for creative activity. Work fits in here as a critical activity that allows not only for the meeting of basic needs but also for the opportunity for creativity and meaningful activity. Beyond enabling people to survive materially, work has the capacity to offer them meaning in their lives. It can also become, as discussed by critics such as Marx, a source of alienation, depending on how it is organized and experienced.

The point is that there are objective aspects to work that make it 'good' or 'bad'. These aspects can be split into extrinsic and intrinsic categories. In the extrinsic category, there is pay. The higher the level of pay, the greater workers' ability to consume effectively in society. Other extrinsic aspects include the level of security in work and the number of hours worked. Workers who work long hours, for example, may face exhaustion and find it difficult to gain meaning from work. Aspects may be interdependent: a high-paid job, for instance, would be experienced as less rewarding under conditions of chronic job insecurity.

The intrinsic rewards from work encompass multiple aspects, most basically the physical and social environment of work. Working conditions may put at risk workers' physical health, or the social relations cultivated at work may make it more meaningful by offering social support – but they can also undermine the meaningfulness of work through forms of abuse or discrimination (e.g. by age, gender, class etc.). There is also the skill content of work. Whether workers can use and develop skills has a direct impact on the qualitative experience of work. The autonomy exercised by workers over work is another critical intrinsic factor. Workers may have the ability to use skills in work, but the quality of their work will be enhanced still further if they also possess the ability to choose when and how to use those skills. The variety and complexity of work are other key factors that determine the intrinsic rewards from work.

These intrinsic factors can offset or accentuate the extrinsic rewards from work. Work that is high-paid, for example, may not be experienced by workers as meaningful where it is performed under oppressive physical conditions or without autonomy. Low-paid and low-skilled work, by contrast, may have the redeeming quality of positive social relations that add vital meaning to work.

I emphasize two points here. Firstly, the above approach to defining the quality of work focuses directly on the characteristics of jobs. It rejects approaches that interpret the quality of work as a signal of subjective feelings gained from work – Bryson and MacKerron's approach is dismissed as being prone to biases and potentially misleading as a basis for understanding the quality of work. Graeber's approach is also rejected, because it focuses largely on survey data to assess the meaning of work. Again, this risks providing a false reading of the extent of the meaningfulness of work that exists in society. Against these approaches, the approach I support here seeks to evaluate the extrinsic and intrinsic aspects of work in particular jobs.

Secondly, specific criteria are laid down to assess the quality of work. This assessment, as outlined above, includes extrinsic and intrinsic dimensions and entails looking beyond subjective data, given that such data can be unreliable as a measure of the quality of work. The focus on the objective characteristics of jobs makes it easier to see when and how jobs fail to meet workers' needs. It can avoid the danger of seeing the move from unemployment into work as always beneficial to workers – indeed, it can be seen how unemployed workers who move into low-quality jobs (e.g. with low pay and low intrinsic rewards) may suffer a loss of well-being. The approach can also show how moves to reform work may be required even where subjective data suggest that workers are satisfied in their jobs or find work meaningful. Finally, it supports improvement in the quality of work generally, not as a way to enhance responses in surveys, but as a way to meet human needs and to promote workers' well-being.

This is not to suggest that data on workers' perceptions of work are useless. Such data, indeed, can help shed light on how workers assess their work and can be useful in measuring particular intrinsic dimensions of work.[40] But these data cannot be used on their own. In short, if research is to understand how well people's lives at work are going (or not going), it needs to explore the objective dimensions of the jobs they do. Notions that equate work with disutility or bullshit jobs, while eye-catching, simply cannot substitute for a more careful and critical scrutiny of the characteristics of jobs that workers are obliged to perform.

I am aware that the definition of the quality of work offered above focuses on the content of jobs. It misses, in this sense, the broader consideration of the objectives to which jobs are directed. The social value of work, as Graeber sees it, is not considered directly. A worker may be well-paid, exercise high skills and retain a high level of autonomy, but she may produce little or no social value. Indeed, her work may potentially harm society – think, for example, of commodity or futures traders (often seen as performing high-quality work), where the objective is to make a financial return, not to serve society. These workers' work has been implicated in creating more unstable and crisis-prone economic conditions – a fact that has tarnished their image in the public realm, though not to such an extent that graduates are unwilling to take up this work. At the opposite extreme, there are hospital cleaners who are low-paid, exercise few skills and have low autonomy, yet perform vital and essential work in keeping hospitals safe. Indeed, this fact may be one redeeming feature of the work they do, offsetting (if only partially) its other negative features.

My response here is twofold. Firstly, my definition of the quality of work focuses importantly on how work matches with workers' needs. This plugs a gap in Graeber's approach, where the characteristics of jobs are obscured. It remains the case that futures traders are better off than hospital cleaners in terms of the quality of work they have to perform. Secondly, the usefulness of work entails a more critical analysis of how work fits into society. Much work is deemed valuable not for what it yields for the quality of workers' lives but for what it contributes to financial goals. This reflects on the imperatives of the capitalist system. The point is that any wider assessment of the meaning of work needs to operate at this system level, not (as Graeber suggests) at the level of responses given to surveys. The other point to make concerns the notion of 'useful work' as defined by William Morris (see the discussion in chapter 2). This notion reflected on the actual content of work – including the capabilities afforded to workers in work – but it also linked work to definite social needs. The goal was to ensure that work was meaningful for workers not just in meeting their own needs but also in fulfilling the needs of society. Making work useful in this respect meant transforming the content of jobs along with the system of work itself.

I return to these issues in chapter 7. Specifically, I will argue for reforms that create a transformation in – and of – work in society. But, in the next chapter, retaining the objective definition of the quality of work presented above, I assess whether high-quality work can be extended to all workers.

5
Demanding Better Work for All

> Work, in its best sense, the healthy energetic exercise of
> faculties, is the aim of life, is life itself.
>
> Alfred Marshall, 'The Future of
> the Working Classes' (1873)

Modern societies feature jobs of different quality. While
some jobs offer work that is high-quality (or good or
meaningful), others provide work that is low-quality (or
bad or meaningless). These differences, as stressed in previous chapters, matter to the lives that people are able to
lead. Workers who perform high-quality work can flourish
and gain some recognition for the work they do, while
those who perform low-quality work can face direct hardship and low status. Questions about inequalities of access
to high-quality work can be used to challenge the way
that work is allocated in society. These inequalities may
exist alongside others linked to the distribution of income
and wealth, and pose major societal problems in need of
resolution.[1]

In this chapter, I assess whether there is scope to extend
the opportunity for better work to all.[2] In the process,
I examine arguments for rejecting the demand to maximize

high-quality work in the economy. These arguments – from mainstream neoclassical economics as well as libertarian philosophy – suggest that individuals should be allowed to 'choose' the work they desire (including work that is low-quality), and rebuff claims for collective interventions to regulate for better work. These arguments also offer an efficiency rationale for maintaining an unequal distribution of the quality of work in society – indeed, they argue that restricting high-quality work to a subset of workers is necessary to meet material needs. Economic progress is linked to the presence and persistence of low-quality work.

My aim in the chapter is to challenge these arguments. I identify flaws in the arguments themselves – including the false view of 'free choice' in labour markets – and present counterarguments that support the case for widening the provision of high-quality work. There is no reason, on efficiency or any other grounds, to prevent the maximum number of workers from achieving work that is high-quality. I argue that the unequal distribution of access to high-quality work in society reflects deeper-lying power imbalances, and that realizing the ideal and goal of high-quality work for all will require broader structural change. The chapter's arguments confirm how the quality of work can be improved upon, and highlight, again in line with the arguments of Marx and Morris, how better work ought to be a central part of a progressive agenda for change in the system of work in society.

Choosing the work we want

It may seem uncontroversial to argue that the quality of work should be enhanced. Surely, it is in the interests of all workers that steps are taken to raise the extrinsic and intrinsic rewards of work? No one, it seems, could deny that society would benefit from regulations to protect and promote higher-quality work?

Some prominent organizations, including many trade unions, have indeed supported the goal of better work. The International Labour Organization, for example, has a 'Decent Work' programme that aims to elevate the quality of work.[3] There are also debates about the merits of improving work's quality in the UK. These debates include arguments that society should aim to ensure the maximum number of people perform 'good work'.[4]

Yet proponents of regulation face certain counterarguments. The latter rest on the idea that workers should be given the option to decide on the work they want to do and should not be hindered by the state or trade unions from achieving their own goals in work. The stress on individual liberty overrides arguments for taking collective action to promote higher-quality work.

That idea is found in mainstream neoclassical economics. As we saw in chapter 3, mainstream economic theory assumes that workers are free to decide the hours they work. Without compulsion to work and occupying the position of 'free agents', workers are assumed to allocate their time to work in a manner that maximizes their utility. This kind of reasoning suggests that collective intervention to regulate work hours should be outlawed – rather, there is an emphasis on workers making rational choices over work time in an unregulated or 'free' labour market.

The same line of argument is applied to workers' choices over the content of work. In mainstream neoclassical economics, workers are assumed to have preferences for work – some workers are assumed to want high-quality work, while others are assumed to want work that pays well.[5] These differences in preferences are not accounted for, but rather are asserted and used in modelling labour supply choices. Those workers wanting high-quality work are assumed to be allocated to employers that can afford to provide such work. In return for meeting their preferences, these workers are assumed to forgo some level of pay – in short, higher-quality work is assumed to command lower wages because some workers want to undertake it.

Workers wanting higher pay and who are indifferent to the quality of work, by contrast, are assumed to be allocated to work that employers cannot afford to improve. As a result, workers are assumed to be paid for the added costs of performing lower-quality work and are seen to be in a position where they can maximize utility.

The above assumptions form part of the economic theory of 'compensating differentials' – a theory that originates in Adam Smith's early writings (see chapter 2), but which has been formalized in modern neoclassical economics. The theory implies certain things. Firstly, it suggests that wages will adjust to compensate for the net costs of working – relative wages will accurately reflect differences in the quality of work between jobs. Secondly, the theory implies that workers are allocated to forms of work that they want to do – free choice is upheld and is used to justify the allocation of workers to different kinds of work. Thirdly, the theory asserts that policies to improve the quality of work are not needed – rather, the quality of work is assumed to be 'optimal' from a choice as well as efficiency perspective. Any attempt to promote higher-quality work by collective intervention, it is argued, will infringe some workers' freedom while adding to employers' costs. The implication is that workers and employers should be granted the freedom to strike bargains in their mutual interests and should not face any restrictions on their behaviour.

This approach is complemented by the theory of human capital. Workers are assumed to make investments in education in order to access paid work. Those who are forward-thinking and invest in knowledge (or human capital) have the prospect of future pay-offs from high-quality work. By contrast, individuals who make the decision not to invest in education and to enter the labour market directly face accessing low-quality work. Human capital theory retains the choice element, assuming that the distribution of work in society reflects rational decisions made by utility-maximizing agents.[6]

The approach taken in mainstream neoclassical economics is echoed in the work of some libertarian philosophers. Robert Nozick, in his book *Anarchy, State, and Utopia*, argues against the idea of regulating for higher-quality work.[7] Nozick's basic view is that workers should be treated as sovereign agents, with their own preferences and views of what is good. Workers, he asserts, want different things from work and are not always motivated by a desire for high-quality work – to the contrary, some workers may be quite prepared to forgo higher-quality work, if it means securing higher pay. Nozick suggests that workers will be compensated for doing low-quality work and upholds workers' freedom to choose the work they desire. He dismisses the idea of state regulation for higher-quality work, and replaces it with a libertarian ideology that asserts individual workers' rights to negotiate with employers over the pay and quality of work.

Nozick considers why high-quality work is not available in all workplaces. He falls back on a simple cost argument. He argues that not all employers can afford to improve the quality of work – rather, many employers find it more cost-effective to provide low-quality work. The higher cost of paying workers to do such work is seen to be less than the additional cost of improving the quality of work. Nozick believes that the work offered in society accords with principles of efficiency, and, in this sense, is not improvable.

The corollary of mainstream neoclassical economics together with libertarian philosophy is that society should accept the inevitability of some low-quality work. This inevitability derives from its inherent efficiency – hence, if this kind of work was eradicated, there would be an increase in firm costs, thereby reducing the scope for progress in output and consumption. If workers do low-quality work, they are fully compensated for performing it and their decisions to do it are, in essence, voluntary. Human capital theory holds that workers perform low-quality work as a result of their previous non-investments in education and training – again, the idea of individual consent is upheld. In all respects, there is support for a world free of regulations, where workers and employers are able to strike mutually beneficial bargains over the allocation of work. Any kind of regulation for higher-quality work is seen as unnecessary and ultimately counterproductive.

The illusion of free choice

The story presented in mainstream neoclassical economics and libertarian philosophy may suit a particular ideology – one conducive to preserving the status quo – but it fails to accord with the realities of choice faced by the majority of workers. In practice, most workers have little choice over the work they do – rather, the nature and quality of work are set for them by the employers who hire them. The fact that employers' interests can (and often do) diverge from those of workers can mean that available work fails to match workers' preferences. Indeed, it can mean that workers are required to do work that they have no interest in and that directly harms them.

The crucial missing element in the approaches reviewed in the last section is the issue of power. The picture painted is of workers meeting employers as equals in the labour market and of bargains being struck that benefit both workers and employers. What is missed is how workers are at a power disadvantage vis-à-vis employers. In reality, employers hire workers, not the other way around. Workers must work in order to live. While workers are not bound to work for any particular employers (capitalism is not slavery), they are still required to take paid work. Once in paid work, workers have no direct say over what work they do and how they do it, but instead must act under conditions that employers dictate. What these power inequalities mean is that low-quality work can be imposed on workers against their wishes and to the detriment of their well-being.

Having committed to paid roles, workers cannot easily switch to other kinds of work. Given the acquisition of specific skills, options to move work may be restricted. But even where skills are generic, the presence of unemployment may bind workers to their existing roles. They may be required to endure work that is incompatible with their preferences. To assume that workers can refuse work if their preferences are not met is to misunderstand how the labour market really works.

The idea that wages vary inversely with the quality of work is also disputable. Low-quality work, in practice, is rewarded with low wages. There is a double penalty for doing low-quality work, namely low intrinsic rewards and low pay. This contrasts with the double benefit (high intrinsic rewards and high wages) that accrues to those in high-quality work. The theory of compensating differentials presented in conventional economics textbooks, in short, has no clear empirical basis.

Once the existence of unequal power is accepted, a different view of the world appears – one in which the presence of high-quality work is contingent not just on cost calculations made by employers, but also on the pressure exerted by workers to secure such work. I indicated in chapter 3 how realizing work time reduction has entailed workers gaining greater bargaining power. Likewise, progress in the quality of work depends on workers pushing employers to improve the quality of work. It is also linked to workers' success in securing state support in enacting laws and regulations that encourage higher-quality work.

Again, while workers may demand improvements in the quality of work, they have no certainty of meeting their demands. Workers may prefer certain things from work while their preferences remain systematically unmet due to their weak bargaining power. Low-quality work, then, may persist because workers lack the power to change it. This lack of power may be explained by the weakness or absence of trade unions. It may also be explained by the lack of any supportive state regulations and laws that promote workers' interests.

Human capital theory, for its part, misses how many people face a lack of opportunity in education and confront discrimination in the labour market that prevents them from getting the work that matches their potential. The idea that people can make rational choices over their education again overlooks the inequalities and imbalances of power that exist in the world and that limit the choices open to people.

The wider point is that stress on individual choice in the context of the allocation of work in society is not only unrealistic but also a distortion of the actual politics of work. It obscures the fact that many workers face direct exploitation and alienation in work. It also ignores how the latter problems call for deeper-level change, not just in the regulation of the labour market, but also in the nature of the system itself. It is impossible to speak of workers gaining high-quality work, in short, without considering how power might be equalized in society.

Adapting to adversity

The arguments from mainstream neoclassical economics and libertarian philosophy outlined above do not enquire into the origins of workers' preferences, but rather imply that workers have independent and exogenous preferences for work that they seek to realize through their choices in the labour market. While some workers have interests in high-quality work, others remain indifferent to such work. This indifference is given by their nature and is not influenced at all by their environment.

This way of theorizing can be disputed. Specifically, workers' preferences are malleable and indeed adaptable to the environment in which they live and work.[8] Workers, for example, may start out with high expectations about work, but over time they may moderate their expectations in line with the work they can actually obtain. The process of adaptation in this instance may mean that workers' preferences are altered – workers may begin with preferences for high-quality work, but because they cannot achieve these preferences, they may come to acquire different preferences that are less demanding of work. Indeed, they may come to prefer simple things – such as having 'a job' or 'earning a living'. These things may be put before other demands such as the desire for autonomy and creative achievement in work.

Other workers, by contrast, may be socialized to see work as just a way to earn money and may prefer work that has few intrinsic rewards – but these preferences reflect more on the workers' background (including potentially their class position) than on their innate desires for work. These workers may not demand much from work and may even register (through surveys) high levels of satisfaction with work (see the related discussion in chapter 4). But again, their demands and reported job satisfaction are a reflection of their socially acquired norms and expectations about work.

Why do adaptation and preference manipulation matter? Firstly, they suggest that workers may come to prefer things that they wish were otherwise. A worker who has to perform low-quality work may come to accept it, but only because she is not able to achieve any better work. The meeting of her preference may simply imply adaptation to adversity – or, in everyday language, it could be seen as a sign of her 'making the best of a bad job'. The mainstream neoclassical economist or libertarian philosopher who interpreted preference fulfilment as a sign of the worker meeting her inner desires would be mistaken. Indeed, they would run the risk of hiding how far the worker in question faces real adversity in work, and in turn, low well-being.

Secondly, such adaptive preferences suggest a more critical treatment of work itself. Rather than infer the quality of work from the decisions that workers make in the labour market, it is important to think more critically about the work that workers actually do. Low-quality work, for example, can be judged as inferior on the basis of what it prevents workers from doing and being in their lives. Again, workers may choose – for adaptive reasons – this kind of work, but this does not mean that the work is to be accepted or condoned. To the contrary, low-quality work can be criticized for disallowing workers from being creative, doing skilful work and being recognized for their efforts. That is, low-quality work can be censured, regardless of what preferences workers may have for it. Further, it is clear that those who perform high-quality work are in a powerful and privileged position, and that their choices represent expanded capabilities that are not open to those who must settle for lower-quality work.

Finally, the existence of adaptive preferences highlights the need for progress in the quality of work. Mainstream neoclassical economists and libertarian philosophers imply that the world of work is perfect as it is. It is perfect to the extent that it represents the fulfilment of choices made by utility-maximizing workers together with profit-maximizing employers. But if preferences are adaptive, work can be criticized on the basis that, while workers' preferences may be met in many cases, these preferences reflect the influence of the environment. This influence is important because it suggests that costs are still being incurred in allocating work and that instances of low-quality work warrant reform. The case for reform is built on the idea that workers' choices over work are limited and that different preferences (ones conducive to the greater provision of higher-quality work) would exist if the quality of work in general was enhanced. The argument would be to reform work in order to counter and overcome the adaptive preferences held by workers.

Power trumps efficiency

Mainstream neoclassical economists and libertarian philosophers argue further that low-quality work is efficient:
employers only adopt the most efficient methods of production and, where low-quality work exists, it reflects
employers' optimal decisions. It follows that, if low-quality
work were to disappear, efficiency would suffer, imposing
higher costs on all in society.

This particular idea once again ignores the role of power
in inhibiting the quality of work. Employers may be able to
achieve improvements in efficiency by enacting policies to
raise the quality of work, but they may forgo these policies
due to a desire to maintain their power over workers.
The issue here is not that high-quality work is unfeasible
economically, but that it is actively resisted by employers
for reasons of power.

There is a long history of scholarship that has shown
how efficiency gains have been trumped by power consid-
erations. The rise of the factory system, for example, has
been linked to capitalist employers' desire to exert control
over workers. Factories were not in any sense the most efficient way to organize work – rather, they were developed
to allow capitalist employers to extend their power over
the labour process.[9] Similarly, technology under capitalism
has been used, not to improve the efficiency of production,
but instead to undermine workers' power to resist control
by capitalist employers.[10] The point is that technology and
the organization of work are not neutral forces, but rather
are shaped by political factors.

This point applies equally to the provision of high-quality
work. Consider, for example, steps taken by employers to
raise workers' autonomy over work. These would offer the
potential to raise the quality of work for workers. Indeed,
workers may be expected to show greater motivation
at work and perhaps even a greater willingness to come
up with new ideas that may lead to higher productivity.

Higher-quality work for workers may coincide with lower unit costs for employers. To be sure, there may be costs for employers in restructuring work to improve workers' autonomy. In a production-line setting, for instance, team-based production methods may be adopted, entailing new investments in plant design. But these costs may be more than offset by greater worker morale and productivity.

Nonetheless, for all the economic benefits on offer, employers may still decide to restrict worker autonomy. Firstly, employers heed the interests of financial stakeholders. The demand for short-term profitability stemming from these stakeholders may lead to forgoing what are seen as costly investments in labour – these could include moves to extend workers' autonomy. Indeed, pressure from financial stakeholders may lead to erosions in the quality of work, from lower pay to poorer working conditions. The interests of financial stakeholders may override those of workers and prevent progress in the quality of work. Secondly, employers may perceive the extension of workers' autonomy over work as a threat. Workers with more autonomy could potentially threaten employers' ability to gain the lion's share of the surpluses generated in production and to manage the labour process. Again, even while improvements in the quality of work could add to efficiency, these may be resisted by employers for reasons linked to their desire for control in the workplace.

The implication here is that efficiency may be restricted in the economy below levels that could be achieved if power was more evenly distributed. The libertarian argument – in economics and philosophy – that employers will focus on maximum efficiency misses how political forces may limit the quality of work, and how inefficiency may persist because employers want to retain their position of power over workers. To believe that employers will pursue higher efficiency without regard to issues of power is naïve at best and a caricature of the realities of work at worst.

The human costs of low-quality work

Mainstream neoclassical economists and libertarian phi-losophers argue too that workers can choose low-quality work without harm to themselves. Not only will workers be compensated for doing this work, they will also be able to lead healthy and contented lives. At least, there is no sense of any cost to workers in performing low-quality work.

Again, this view can be challenged. There is much evidence that low-quality work damages workers' health and well-being. This suggests the need for reform, even where workers notionally consent to do low-quality work.

Recall the criticism that Adam Smith levelled against the division of labour (see discussion in chapter 2). He recognized that the division of labour was essential in raising productivity and economic growth, yet he deplored its human consequences. Workers' minds would be destroyed by their being exposed to the same tasks on a repeated basis. Smith openly acknowledged that low-quality work was a cost of economic progress, though he did not regard the cost as too high. Rather, it would be compensated by the economic bounty of higher output and consumption. Here he anticipated modern arguments that suggest low-quality work is efficient and ultimately unavoidable.

Smith failed to see how the persistence of dehumanizing work might be a cause of lower productivity. The spread of unintelligent work would harm productivity by limiting employers' ability to tap into workers' ingenuity and creativity. Further, productivity would be harmed by the erosion of workers' morale. But the deeper problem with Smith's approach was that it placed productivity ahead of workers' well-being. There was a one-sided focus on economic goals. These goals were clearly important, but the focus on them was at the expense of seeing ways to protect and promote the qualitative experience of work.

Smith realized the human costs of the division of labour, without recognizing the importance of their resolution, not indirectly via years of schooling, but directly through the reform of work.

Research has confirmed Smith's concerns about the negative effects of low quality. Workers, for example, have been shown to suffer losses in cognitive ability through exposure to simple and non-stimulating forms of work.[11] These losses are difficult to recover from and can lead to erosions of both labour productivity and the quality of leisure time. In certain cases, mindless work can provide the basis for mindless leisure.[12] Other research has shown how workers in jobs with low levels of autonomy are more prone to physical illnesses such as heart attacks and to premature death (see the discussion in chapter 4).[13] Finally, one recent study linked forms of precarious work that feature unstable work schedules to 'psychological distress, poor sleep quality and unhappiness'.[14]

This reinforces the point that, even where workers say they prefer low-quality work (for adaptive or non-adaptive reasons), its existence can still be criticized. Indeed, society as a whole can benefit from taking steps to improve such work. The benefits would be measured not just in improved well-being, but also in lower health-care costs and potentially higher productivity.

Equalizing the distribution of high-quality work

In the discussion above, I have established that arguments against improving the quality of work – based on choice and efficiency claims – do not stand up to close scrutiny. Is there a case for extending high-quality work to the maximum number of workers? As I will show below, there are six arguments that suggest this case cannot be sustained and that offer support for a world where high-quality work is unevenly distributed. My intention is to counter these arguments and to support the case for a more equal distribution of high-quality work.

A *first argument* for restricting access to high-quality work returns to the efficiency argument made above. It suggests that to widen access to high-quality work would bring unacceptable losses in efficiency, because high or maximum efficiency requires that some workers perform low-quality work. As seen above, this was the argument made by Adam Smith – he defended the division of labour on the basis that it raised efficiency levels, and this economic benefit more than offset the negative effects of the proliferation of low-quality work. Modern mainstream economics makes similar claims in terms of restricting workers' autonomy. It assumes that workers will 'shirk' the effort and responsibility of work, and justifies controls to limit workers' autonomy on the basis that these will raise efficiency levels. In efficiency wage theory, for example, unemployment is judged as an effective way to ensure higher productivity.[15] Further, in transaction cost economics, forms of hierarchy are seen as the efficient solution to the problem of worker opportunism within organizations.[16]

The counter to the above argument is that work can be redesigned. Smith, as we have seen, limited his focus to the division of labour, believing that the separation of workers into individual tasks was the only way to meet society's material needs. My response is that the design and implementation of the division of labour are adaptable – even in a production-line context, workers can self-control the production process and input ideas into the way that work is carried out. And where a strict division of labour is required, technology could be used instead of labour, freeing up workers to do other, more interesting and intellectually stimulating work. Ideas of efficiency in the workplace need not begin and end with workers being restricted to particular tasks – instead, they may be expanded to include different arrangements that allow for and encourage workers' skill and autonomy, and in turn, embed higher-quality work.

Modern mainstream economics misses how cooperation and trust can be secured by granting workers more
autonomy over work – efficiency can be raised alongside
improvement in the quality of work. The focus on shirking
behaviour and direct control implies a trade-off between
efficient production and high work quality, when in practice, the two goals can – and should – be combined.

A *second argument* relates to profitability. Firms may
want to improve the quality of work, but by doing so, they
would erode profits and possibly even go bankrupt. The
viability of firms, then, depends on their maintaining some
low-quality work. This revives the view of mainstream
neoclassical economists and libertarian philosophers on
economic barriers to high-quality work. But profit con-
siderations may conceal issues of power maintenance (see
above discussion). Profits may be increased despite the use
of inefficient technology and work organization. Further,
consider whether and to what extent firms can achieve
profits by other routes – if low-quality work leads to lower
worker morale and cooperation (with higher rates of
absenteeism), then its economic cost may be high. Again,
employers may prefer to maintain low-quality work for
other (power) reasons, but this need not rule out their
raising profits by extending opportunities for high-quality
work. Indeed, a large part of the management literature has
attempted to show how progress in profitability and work
quality can be achieved simultaneously.[17] Whether this
literature is viewed as convincing is not the crucial issue.
Rather, the point is that there is some scope – however
limited – to improve profits with higher-quality work.

A *third argument* refers back to the preference-based
claim that some workers want to do low-quality work.
This implies that work is inconsequential to workers' lives
and that, despite the distresses workers might face at work
(from direct oppression to sweated labour), they can still
lead lives of joy and meaning. This peculiar type of argument is, then, used to defend a situation where only a
fraction of the population are able to achieve high-quality

work. Here again, I think the argument misses how preferences are adaptive and how workers may come to prefer things through lack of better alternatives. Further, it neglects how low-quality work can be directly harmful to workers. Accumulated evidence (see above) shows how low-quality work is bad for human health and the quality of life – whether preferred or not, low-quality work should be minimized. The argument also shows a remarkable indifference to goals beyond just earning money from work. Specifically, there is no sense of how the quality of work might be improved and how progress in society means resolving distresses in work, not just accumulating more things for people to consume.

A *fourth argument* against the idea that high-quality work can be extended to all workers is that some forms of work are inherently bad or low-quality and that to suggest all workers can perform high-quality work is to ignore the existence of these forms. Think, for example, of dirty and degrading work, from cleaning toilets to working on an assembly line. Such work is needed to meet society's needs and it is utopian to imagine that it can be avoided.

My response is straightforward. If necessary work is too bad for human workers to perform, then it should be eliminated as far as possible. This entails using technology to reduce bad work. One fault of the present system is that it has limited capacity to harness technology in order to alleviate the costs of work – to the contrary, technology progresses almost despite its effects on the quality of work. But this simply reflects the system's imperatives and limits – there is no reason why technology cannot be reharnessed to remove drudgery. This was the aim of past thinkers such as Marx and Keynes and ought to be revived in the present, against arguments that say low-quality work is inevitable.[18]

Where low-quality work cannot be replaced with technology, then more creative ways need to be found to reduce its burden. For example, low-quality work could be rotated among workers, so that no one group of workers would be subject to this kind of work all of the time; rather, its burden would be shared out. Rotating work in this way would help to reduce the stigma attached to doing low-quality work and would also create a wider awareness of the need to reduce unpleasant work.[19] In particular, if everyone did their share of low-quality work, there would be a greater appreciation of the sacrifices made by those undertaking such work and of the necessity of reducing time spent in it. One could even imagine a kind of civic responsibility attached to doing unpleasant work, as a service that everyone must carry out on behalf of the community.

This solution fits with ideas set out by William Morris (see chapter 2). Realizing it would entail radical shifts in society. In particular, low-quality work would need to be allocated across workers – new or augmented workers' councils, for example, might be formed to decide on the allocation, with democratic participation facilitated and encouraged through joint decision-making. The goal would be to develop norms of reciprocity and cooperation in work allocation, with the sharing out of low-quality work accepted as a necessary and desirable part of society.

Finally – again following Morris – society might decide to forgo some output by not performing low-quality work. The sacrifice of output, in this case, might be judged a price worth paying for a higher quality of work. Once more, this would imply radical change, with the improvement in the quality of work put ahead of the increase in output.

A *fifth argument* opposing the idea that high-quality work can be extended to all workers is that high-quality work must be restricted to a few workers in society because this is the only way to realize the benefits of job specialization. Medical doctors and university lecturers, for example, can only be effective at practising medicine and delivering lectures, respectively, if they devote all their time to one kind of work. If work is restricted on the grounds of job specialization, then there will be limited scope to widen access to high-quality work – indeed, the result may be a highly uneven distribution of high-quality work, though one that society has to accept for reasons of promoting skill and expertise in particular occupations.

My response is that, while job specialization has its place, there is scope to alter the workplaces in which the jobs are done. Doctors may specialize in medicine but still be afforded the same decision-making rights as nurses and other workers in a hospital. Lecturers, too, may specialize in lecturing but still take the same position in the university hierarchy as other workers. Flattening the structure of organizations can help to create more democratic conditions where the voice of every worker is respected and where scope for autonomy is widened. Job specialization is no barrier to enhancing the quality of work within organizations.

Further, it can be argued that those who have 'expert' roles, from doctors to lecturers, should do some drudge work. A form of work rotation might be envisaged where those filling these roles combine their main work with other kinds of work that are less satisfying. University lecturers, for example, might be required to clean their offices, creating more time for others to do more rewarding work.[20] The point is that, in return for their favoured position in society, those in high-quality work should take their share of low-quality work. Work-sharing, allied with more democratic work organization, would help to extend opportunities for high-quality work to a greater number of people.

A *sixth argument* against extending high-quality work to all is more controversial. It suggests that some people cannot do high-quality work because of their alleged inferior abilities. This argument draws strength from biased and prejudicial claims that some people are born with the capability to do only low-quality work.

This argument can be challenged head on. In reality, many people lack opportunity to secure higher-quality work not because of their innate ability but because of inability to access adequate training and education. Gaps in the training and education system disempower some people and put them on a track where low-quality work is the only option available. But lack of opportunity reflects embedded social and economic disadvantage linked to factors such as class and race. It is clear that with more equal access to training and education more people could secure better work.

The wider point here is that barriers to workers gaining higher-quality work are imposed not by nature but by the kind of society in which we live.[21] There is scope to overcome disadvantage and realize individual talents and skills by reforming society. Many workers may be restricted to low-quality work in the present. But there is no reason why these restrictions cannot be overcome and the opportunity for higher-quality work be extended to the maximum number of people.

Justice in work

The distribution of work matters. If some people in society cannot gain access to high-quality work and have to accept low-quality work, their life-chances as well as health and well-being can be expected to suffer. Not only will they be likely to face low wages – they will also lack the opportunity to enjoy the direct benefits that high-quality work brings. These benefits include the opportunity for self-development in work, but also extend to the status that comes from doing high-quality work. This inequality has led some writers to highlight the importance of injustice in work and to call for progress towards 'contributive justice', maximizing the provision of high-quality work. These writers argue that society cannot be truly just until high-quality work is open to all.[22]

As argued above, potential barriers to enlarging access to high-quality work are surmountable. There is no necessary reason why high-quality work should be hoarded by a few in society. Rather, there is a compelling case, on

economic and moral grounds, for increasing the amount
and smoothing the distribution of work that is high-quality.

But why is high-quality work not more widely available
in society? The answer can be found in the structure of
work in society. Fundamentally, workers are too weak
relative to employers to achieve high-quality work. For
all the talk of equality in markets and freedom to choose
that is espoused by some mainstream commentators, most
workers lack the power to improve the quality of work.
Injustice in work, in essence, reflects the existence and
persistence of unequal power.

Consider the capitalist employment relationship. Work
in capitalist society is imposed as opposed to chosen.
Workers have little say over what work they do – rather,
they face taking work that is shaped by employers' interests. The deficit of high-quality work is to be expected, not
least because of the benefits that accrue to employers from
maintaining low-quality work.

But, in recent decades, changes in capitalism have influenced the extent of high-quality work. In the past, trade
unions helped to secure better work for workers, in part,
by blocking off low routes to higher profitability based on
lower wages and higher work intensity, but also by winning concessions from employers, including shorter work
hours, improved working conditions and greater democracy at work. The decline of trade unions in countries such
as the UK and US has set back the cause of higher-quality
work – indeed, this decline has contributed to eroding the
quality of work.

Wider shifts in firm governance and in politics have
also played a part. As discussed in chapter 3, firms have
become more focused on maximizing shareholder value – a
fact that has compromised the quality of work. National
governments have, likewise, put the interests of capital
ahead of those of labour, by hollowing out welfare states
and by resisting new labour reforms.

The crucial point is that injustice in work has persisted
as capitalist economies have advanced. In the present, the

effects of crisis have made it more difficult for workers to achieve higher-quality work. Indeed, crisis itself has put many workers in a position where they have had to accept a declining quality of work to remain in employment.

Returning to the arguments above, preferences have remained adaptive. In the context where workers cannot get the work they want, preferences have been lowered to meet the lack of high-quality work. The apparent lack of resistance to lower-quality work may be interpreted by libertarians as proof of workers not wanting higher-quality work when in reality it reflects workers adjusting to circumstances where high-quality work is in short supply.

This point reinforces the need to uncover and challenge the bases of unequal power in society and to repudiate arguments that justify denying the majority in society high-quality work. By developing more critical agendas about the concentration of power and the possibilities for change, there is scope to raise awareness of the need for, and benefit of, increasing the supply and equalizing the distribution of high-quality work. There are clear ways to realize this need and benefit, via collective action. Before I address issues of reform, I examine in the next chapter the scope for technology to affect the volume and quality of work.

6

Automation and a World without Work

Modern methods of production have given us the possibility of ease and security for all; we have chosen, instead, to have overwork for some and starvation for the others. Hitherto we have continued to be as energetic as we were before there were machines; in this we have been foolish, but there is no reason to go on being foolish for ever.

Bertrand Russell, 'In Praise of Idleness' (1935)

The last few years have seen a revival of interest in the topic of automation. Several high-profile books have appeared on the topic, fuelling wider concern in the media and policy realms about the possibilities for technology to automate work.[1] These books, in turn, have drawn on evidence that suggests capitalist societies face a new era of technological progress.[2] It is claimed that, in the so-called 'Second Machine Age' or 'Fourth Industrial Revolution' that capitalism has now entered, machines (or robots) will increasingly replace human workers in work. In the coming world, work will be in short supply and people's lives will entail more time away from it.

The possible demise of work has elicited a mixed response. On the one hand, it has sparked concern at the prospect of rising unemployment and higher inequality. The challenge of the future, from this perspective, will be how to manage the technological transition in ways that prevent mass unemployment and a more unequal distribution of income.[3] Yet, on the other hand, it has prompted visions of a better future – one where people can live better lives without work. Some post-work perspectives, indeed, take the optimistic view that automation can liberate humanity from work and create the basis for a new leisure society. Automation, on this view, should be accelerated and used to expand free time.[4]

This chapter addresses the modern debate on automation from a critical perspective. It questions whether work will disappear through automation, and argues that technology under capitalism poses a much greater threat to the quality of work than its quantity. Further, it examines responses to the perceived automation risk, and links these to ideas about the nature of work and ways of living well without work. Finally, the chapter considers the politics of automation – in particular, it argues that reforms in ownership are vital if automation is ever to deliver for the majority in society.

Machine dreams

The idea that technology will replace workers in production has been repeated in economic and political thought. Specific worries have persisted that technology will lead to job losses and lower wages. Infamously, in the early nineteenth century, the Luddites smashed the machinery that was seen to threaten their jobs and livelihoods. Subsequently, a Luddite-like fear around the negative effects of technology on employment and wages has recurred.[5] There has also been a concern that technology will undermine the quality of work. Marx, as was shown in chapter 2, stressed how – beyond raising unemployment – labour-saving technology under capitalism would tend to produce more alienating work. Capitalist employers would gain from technological progress, at the expense of workers' poverty and alienation.

But there has also been a vision of a world where technology operates to enhance well-being and freedom in society. The classical economists, from Adam Smith to J. S. Mill, may have bemoaned the disruptive effects of technology on workers' lives, but they still believed in its essential positive value – technology would offer net benefits to society in the long run and had to be allowed to develop. Even critics like Mill, who thought that technology was adding to drudgery and lengthening work time, retained the belief that technology would – under the right conditions – deliver a better future.[6]

Marx, again as we saw in chapter 2, may have criticized how technology was being used under capitalism, but he stressed the possibilities for technology to be used for good in a future socialist society. The vision of reharnessing technology – of putting it to use in realizing human goals – was at the heart of his depiction of a better society. Indeed, for Marx, part of the promise of socialism was that it would enable technology to be used in ways that would add to the quality of work and life. He stressed, though, the need for a revolution in society and the move beyond capitalism.

In 1930, as was mentioned in chapter 3, Keynes predicted that 'technological unemployment' would increase over time, though this increase would help to enhance workers' lives by freeing them to perform creative activities outside of work. In the 1950s and 1960s, disparate voices, from the politician Richard Nixon to the novelist Isaac Asimov, foresaw a reduction of work through the continuous development of technology. Keynes's prediction was set to be realized and humanity would face the prospect of working less in the future. Unlike Keynes, however, some were concerned that technology might leave people without purpose and meaning in their lives.[7] Similarly, during the 1990s, some commentators could be found predicting the 'end of work'.[8] The seeming fact that work hours were stagnating and employment levels were high failed to dent this view. Rather, the idea persisted that work was in terminal decline and that humanity must prepare itself for a future without work.

Modern debate builds on past contributions, but also seeks to deliver a novel message, namely that 'this time will be different'. In the past, technology has proceeded in a way that has allowed work to persist. Past predictions of the decline of work made by Keynes and others have been falsified – in reality, work has continued, at the same time as technology has advanced (see chapter 3). Yet the argument is now made that technology will – finally – erode work. While work may have survived up to now, in the future it will succumb to technology. In particular, new digital technologies (including artificial intelligence and machine learning) will create the opportunity to replace work that has previously survived automation and, as a result, workers will lose their ability to compete against machines. The prospect, then, is of a future where work will effectively run out and where humans will be faced with having to find other things than work to fill their time.

Different concrete examples are given to illustrate the possibilities for automation. Driverless cars are one example. It was once thought that the task of driving a car could not be automated; however, there are now driverless cars in development and in use on public roads, and the prospect of their wider adoption in the future promises a reduction in driving-based jobs, from taxi driver to trucker. It is claimed that automation will not just threaten low-skilled work but will also pose challenges for higher-skilled work. For example, the wider use of digital technologies in legal practice will threaten the jobs of some legal workers.[9]

The suggestion is that digital technologies will keep on advancing and that, while some jobs will persist, the scope for these jobs to continue will erode through time. It is not a matter of if jobs will disappear, but when and in what number.[10] The onus is, then, on policy-makers to prepare for the coming 'world without work'. Debate mainly focuses on the speed and timing of mass automation, rather than on its potential non-achievement. Again, the expectation is that the days of working for a living are numbered and that the future will bring forth more leisure.

Empirical evidence has fuelled the impression that many millions of jobs are 'at risk' of automation. In their influential study, Carl Frey and Michael Osborne suggest that 47 per cent of existing jobs could be automated in the US by the earlier 2030s. Estimates for the UK suggest that fifteen million jobs could disappear due to automation – this approximates to half of the current workforce.[11] In developing and emerging countries, the estimates of potential job losses are even higher – for example, more than two-thirds of jobs in India and over three-quarters of jobs in China are seen to be vulnerable to automation.[12]

Estimates, of course, are heavily caveated. Frey and Osborne, for example, highlight several 'engineering bottlenecks' that might inhibit the automation of jobs. Building on their research, other authors have offered lower estimates of potential job losses from automation.[13] But debate at an empirical level has not shifted the underlying view that jobs will become more susceptible to automation and that, in the future, most workers will be robots, as opposed to humans. Rather, based on the belief that technological change will accelerate, the view is that mass automation will occur in the years ahead.

Responses to the prospect of automation vary. One perspective worries that technology will cause significant disruption and that it should be managed under current conditions. Erik Brynjolfsson and Andrew McAfee, for example, suggest that automation, if left unmanaged, will create a more unequal and divided society.[14] From their perspective, the 'bounty' of automation – its ability to improve living standards and potentially add to the quality of work – is threatened by a widening in the 'spread', with the rich becoming richer at the expense of the rest of society. In response, the authors argue that society should implement new policies to enable workers to reskill and keep pace with the latest technology. In their view, the Second Machine Age can be managed successfully under capitalism, so long as policy-makers equip workers with the right education and skills to 'race with machines'.

A more radical perspective, by contrast, links automation to the move to a post-work future. Nick Srnicek and Alex Williams, in particular, argue for 'full automation' as a way to bring forward a workless future.[15] From this perspective, the acceleration of technology is welcomed and seen to form the basis for a fundamentally new society where people are liberated from work. This line of argument is situated in a broader critique of work under capitalism.

The point is that, across the political spectrum, there is a common belief that technological progress will lead to the reduction of work in society. The debate is not over whether technology will accelerate, but how to manage its effects. In particular, there is a concern over whether accelerating technology (and with it, declining work opportunities) means preserving capitalism or creating a society beyond it. For more mainstream writers, automation can be achieved – to the benefit of all – under a reformed capitalism. For radical writers, by contrast, automation creates the opportunity to move to a post-capitalist system and to realize a future of less or even zero work. As I show below, however, the apparent consensus over the progress of technology – and its effects on work – can be challenged.

Technology, automation and the quality of work

The idea that technology will propel society to a future without work poses self-evident questions. Most obviously, in the present, much work still exists. While unemployment remains a problem for some, this reflects less on the effects of technology and more on the impacts of policy (including, in the recent past, the embrace of austerity policies by national governments). COVID-19 has also shown starkly how unemployment can be created by factors other than technology. The broader point is that the modern debate on automation obscures the fact that work remains a key activity in society and one that cannot be easily erased.[16]

Further, the future is uncertain. To say that technology will progress and take jobs is to paint a deterministic picture. In reality, there are doubts about both the progress of technology and the disappearance of work. Certainly, there is no reason to expect that technology will eliminate work and produce a workless future. To the contrary, technology is more likely to reshape the quality of work than to reduce its volume. I will make three comments here to illustrate these points.

The first comment concerns barriers to automation. For automation to accelerate, firms will have to make large investments in technology. Yet in many capitalist economies, investment levels remain limited. The relative cheapness of labour makes it economical for firms to retain labour-intensive methods of production and service delivery, while the pursuit of shareholder value means that firms face pressures to cut costs. These pressures can manifest themselves in lower levels of investment, including in new technology. Given the economic and institutional constraints on investment and technology adoption, it cannot be assumed that investment will increase and eliminate jobs across firms.[17]

The second comment relates to the capacity of technology to generate new sources of work. Most obviously, there are the numerous jobs created in the manufacture, distribution, design and retail of technology.[18] Take the example of the smartphone. Far from eliminating employment, it has created many new jobs. These jobs form part of large value chains, stretching from poorer nations in the global South to richer nations in the global North. Jobs, too, have been created through firms' marketing efforts

– smartphones have offered new platforms to market things to consumers, helping to support higher levels of demand, and in turn, higher levels of output. With advances in technology likely to create new areas for advertising and further product development, higher demand levels may be sustained into the future, preventing falls in employment. Moreover, technological progress (by raising productivity) could help to cheapen available goods and services, providing a further boost to consumption. Historically, the productivity effect of technology has helped to raise demand levels and sustain employment. Those predicting the demise of work through automation miss the way in which technology can enlarge work and keep people working and spending in the same ways as at present.

Thirdly, there is scope for technology to advance while the number of low-quality jobs increases. Although current debate focuses on transformed futures of work, the advance of technology may simply mean that many people stay in work, but enjoy fewer benefits from work itself.

The dynamic under capitalism is to keep workers working and consuming.[19] The use of technology to extend marketing opportunities fits with the goal of maintaining work and consumption. But there is also the use and manipulation of technology to secure new ways of working. The drive to lower costs for capital can lead to the automation of functions and the displacement of labour, but it can also create new work in its wake, partly by increasing the incentive to hire labour. To the extent that technology widens the pool of available labour by creating more undifferentiated forms of work, it can place downward pressure on wages in ways that make it more attractive for employers to keep hiring labour. Indeed, reducing wages may thwart investment in technology where it is deemed non-economical. Think, for example, of hand car washes in the UK and fruit picking in the US – old ways of working that could be automated, but persist because there is cheap labour available for capital to hire. If workers' bargaining power is already low due to the decline in trade unions and a more hostile, 'business-friendly' policy environment, then their power is likely to fall even further with the processes of automation. Yet, in this case, workers will face not unemployment, but rather lower-quality jobs.

Technology is already being used and applied in ways that are detrimental to workers. Take modern employment platforms such as Amazon's Mechanical Turk and TaskRabbit. These platforms, enabled by technology, have permitted employers to outsource work at lower cost than if they undertook it internally. Work has been created that bypasses existing labour laws and social protections. Employers, by hiring at a distance and without any formal employment contract, have tended to overlook their moral responsibilities towards workers. A corollary is that employment platforms have been criticized for creating more low-paid, unregulated and insecure work.[20] The prospect of their growth in the future promises to further erode the quality of work open to workers.

The rise of firms like Uber and Deliveroo as part of the so-called 'gig economy' is yet another example of how the latest technology has been combined with inferior labour market practices.[21] The use of technology to create a disposable workforce with fewer labour entitlements has benefitted those owning the companies at the expense of those they hire. In particular, it has meant for workers extended hours of work, without the benefit of sick pay, holiday pay and minimum wages. While often trumpeted as offering 'flexibility' to workers, work in the gig economy has become a means to erode and undermine workers' hard-won rights. Even while workers have secured better terms and conditions, they have done so only via active struggle and against employers' pressure to maintain the status quo.[22]

Further, technology has also been used within workplaces to tighten up monitoring and intensify work. Many workers now face having their actions recorded and assessed by technology on a moment-by-moment basis. They also face monitoring and work outside of normal hours through the use of email and forms of digital scheduling that require workers to be 'on call' around the clock. Critics point to the creation of a new form of 'digital Taylorism' with workers subject to a more intrusive and intensive work environment.[23]

Consider work inside Amazon warehouses. The rise of online shopping – again linked to the use of technology – has led to the growth of these warehouses. Within them, large numbers of workers are employed. Despite being termed 'fulfilment centres', Amazon warehouses have become places of oppression. Not only have workers faced work on short-term and insecure contracts but they have also confronted high levels of monitoring and work intensity. Technology has been used to speed up work. The result has been that workers have suffered high levels of stress and also illness through work. One report, for example, suggested that workers were falling ill and suffering injuries through their exposure to work in some automated Amazon warehouses.[24] There have also been stark reports of Amazon workers being 'forced to urinate in plastic bottles because they could not go to the toilet' during their shift.[25]

The point is that technology has not aided workers in securing better work but rather has become a means to exploit and oppress them. The fault does not lie with technology itself but rather with how it is used. Specifically, as in Amazon warehouses, technology has been used to increase the intensity and burden of work – this has benefitted the owners of Amazon, but it has come at the cost of the well-being and health of workers employed inside its warehouses. Indeed, it has led to harsh and unhealthy work conditions.

The prospect of more sophisticated surveillance technology that can be worn by and even implanted into workers suggests that there will be even greater scope in the future to monitor and intensify work. The fear, in this instance, is less about robots replacing work and more about work being turned into a robot-like experience that is ever more burdensome. As one commentator put it, the concern is that 'humans are being crunched into a robot system working at a robot rate'.[26] If technology proceeds with regard merely to minimizing cost, workers' well-being and health can only continue to suffer.

In summary, a problem with predictions of work's demise, from both mainstream and radical perspectives, is that they fail to see how technology can progress while work is maintained. They miss, in other words, the scope for capitalism to reproduce work and prevent its reduction. A further problem is that they ignore or understate the threats to the quality of work posed by technology and the capacity for low-quality work to persist and even multiply alongside technological progress. The focus on work disappearing can become a distraction from other pressing problems created by technology as it is used and implemented in capitalist society. I now turn to responses to automation, beginning with concern about people's ability to live well without work.

A lament for work

Recall that for Keynes the promise of a better future – facilitated by investment in technology – corresponded to the opportunity to work less (see chapter 3). The vision of an automated world was to be embraced as a means to extend people's freedom to live creative lives outside of work. Keynes was led to this view by a belief in the inherent costs of work – because work was always bad, people would thrive if machines could replace them in work. The counterview is that work can offer certain benefits and that its loss, via automation, may be costly for workers and society more generally. This suggests that automation should be managed in ways that allow workers to continue working.

Brynjolfsson and McAfee take this view. They refer to work itself as 'beneficial'. Citing the words of Voltaire, they state that: 'Work saves a man from three great evils: boredom, vice, and need.' Beyond providing income, work offers the basis for people to participate in positive activity and contribute to society. As the authors stress, in modern society, work provides the benefits of 'self-worth, community, engagement, healthy values, structure, and dignity'.[27] In their view, automating work will not only inflict harm on workers by reducing their well-being – it will also impose high costs on society. They cite evidence on the negative impacts of unemployment on subjective well-being, and on the reduced years of life of those living in areas of high unemployment, to justify their case.

Based on the above ideas, Brynjolfsson and McAfee reject a UBI as a response to automation. A UBI, they argue, only offers workers income – it does not offer the work that workers and society needs to thrive. Rather, they support policies aimed at generating more work – it should be created, even while technology is advancing. The challenge for policy-makers is to make workers employable, so that they can access work that will remain available in the future. Better training and education, in particular, will help workers to fill jobs where human skills remain in demand. But workers themselves will need to take the initiative in finding new sources of work – for example, workers can look to be entrepreneurial and start their own businesses.[28] Brynjolfsson and McAfee's broader vision is based on protecting work and ensuring that the established work economy is maintained in the Second Machine Age.

There are two critical responses to Brynjolfsson and McAfee's perspective. Firstly, they make no acknowledgement of how technology might help to curtail work hours. Brynjolfsson and McAfee neglect the benefits of reducing work time and seem to stick to a view of the world in which full-time work remains the norm. Any vision of increasing time away from work is eclipsed by a narrow focus on maintaining the same work routine. This fact shows how they depart from Keynes's past vision and ignore the evidence that many workers desire and need (for health and other reasons) shorter work hours.[29]

Secondly, the focus on the benefits of work comes at the expense of considering the costs of work. There is no awareness of how workers might face hardship in work and how technology might be adding to this hardship. Brynjolfsson and McAfee use the example of an Amazon warehouse worker to show how 'pride' can be felt in work and offer this as confirmation of the merits of working over not working.[30] They pay no attention to the oppressive working conditions in Amazon warehouses and the costs borne by workers within them. More generally, the authors overlook how work might be costly to workers and how technology might be used not to create and extend work, but instead to reduce its burdens. The idea of securing better work is obscured by an obsession with creating any kind of work. The assumption that all work is good or virtuous drives this obsession and prevents consideration of ways to resolve the direct and opportunity costs of work.

The irony is that, for all the talk of revolutionary change in society, Brynjolfsson and McAfee offer workers little hope for change in their lives at work. Far from promising change, these authors seem to want to prop up the present work system and to reject more radical reforms. The promise of automation is reduced to continued working, without much opportunity for workers to gain freedom from the distresses of work or the ability to enjoy a life beyond it. Again, this is a long way from Keynes's original vision.

Automating drudgery

Post-work writers, as was highlighted above, take a radically different stance from Brynjolfsson and McAfee, arguing that work should be eliminated or 'abolished'.[31] They adopt the view that work is a barrier to human well-being and support automation as a way to free people from drudgery. A negative view of work drives a vision of a future society where humans are replaced in work by machines and where the human freedom to live without work is maximized.

This approach seeks to privilege the elimination of work over its transformation. The laudable effort to automate drudgery eclipses the equally beneficial goal of enhancing the quality of work. These writers neglect how technology might be used to create more opportunity to work with pleasure and meaning. Recall that for William Morris one benefit of technology was that it could be used to reduce pain in work. But he saw too how technology could free people to undertake pleasurable work. Post-work discourse, in short, neglects the role that automation can – and should – play in meeting workers' needs for a positive work experience.[32]

This is not to glorify work and seek its perpetuation. As argued above, those defending work miss both the actual costs of work and the need for work time reduction. Rather, I hold that in saving society from drudgery, technology can also liberate people to work better. Post-work authors, at points, recognize that work can be improved. Some authors, indeed, invoke Morris's writings and signal how the improvement of work can be achieved alongside the reduction of work time.[33] My point here is that, in evaluating the possibilities for automation, this emphasis on the need for, and benefit of, improving the quality of work should be more prominent. A critical discourse on automation, in the end, must offer ways to rethink and recreate work beyond the forms it takes under present-day capitalism.

Ownership matters

The issue of ownership has been surprisingly neglected in the modern debate on automation and the future of work. The tendency has been to stress the power of computers over the power of social agents to shape technology. Yet this issue strikes at the heart of the problems of technology in the present and the possibilities that exist for the repurposing of technology in the future.

Technology is not neutral (see also chapter 5). Rather, it is influenced by the politics of work. Under capitalism, technology is driven by the imperatives of profitability – capitalist employers make investments in technology in order to make higher profits. The objective of profit-making takes precedence over other goals, including ones linked to shortening work time and raising the quality of work. The point is that existing capitalist social relations set constraints on the development and use of technology. Indeed, they threaten to perpetuate forms of technology that will keep people not only working long hours, but also in jobs that are dull, exploitative and potentially dangerous for their health. Recent developments such as the rise of Amazon and Uber reveal the biases and limits to technological progress in modern capitalist societies.

But circumstances do not have to remain this way. There is scope to change how technology is owned and controlled. More directly, workers could have more of a say over how technology is developed and used. Democratizing technology can be seen as a way to make the process and effects of technological innovation more equalitarian.

One author has written that 'who owns the robots rules the world'.[34] Society has less to fear from robots if workers are able to share in the rewards that accrue from their use. One problem, again, of modern society is that the returns from technology are unevenly spread, meaning technological progress coincides with the persistence (and indeed increase) of inequality. Giving workers stakes in the firms in which they work would help to mitigate the threats of automation – in this case, workers would be more able to adjust their hours of work in line with the productivity gains achieved from technological adoption. But if workers could control technology more directly and influence its direction more clearly, that might enable them to effect changes that not only reduce work hours but also improve the quality of work.

The point is that who owns and controls technology matters. Unequal ownership prevents the use of technology for positive outcomes in the present. But the move to more democratic forms of ownership and governance could help to achieve less and better work in the future. As I show in the next chapter, reforms to achieve such a future will require radical change in society.

7

Working for Change

Laborious employment is a calamity now because it is imperiously prescribed upon men as the condition of their existence, and because it shuts them out from a fair participation in the means of knowledge and improvement. When it shall be rendered in the strictest sense voluntary, when it shall cease to interfere with our improvement, and rather become part of it, or at worse be converted into a source of amusement and variety, it may then be no longer a calamity, but a benefit.

William Godwin, *Political Justice* (1793)

The vision of a better future – one where material needs can be met with less necessary work and more creative activity – has inspired thinkers through time. Marx and Keynes, to name two key thinkers, sought to articulate such a vision (see the discussion in chapters 2 and 3). Critical reflection on the future of society has been twinned with criticism of the dominant capitalist system as a potential and actual fetter on progress. Such reflection, in turn, has prompted calls for the rebuilding of society and the creation of post-capitalist futures.

Similar visionary thinking has resurfaced in the present. One reason for this revival, as discussed in chapter 6, is the prospect of automation and the possible disappearance of work – the notion that society is set to face a future without work has generated fresh speculation on different futures, including ones beyond capitalism. But debate about the scope and need for change has also been sparked by the recurrence of crises. The COVID-19 crisis, in particular, has prompted critical thinking about capitalism's capacity to meet people's needs. In the context of the pandemic, with 'normal' life suspended, the parameters for debate on alternative futures have expanded greatly. Time will tell whether the crisis induced by COVID-19 will lead to any wider change in society.

In this chapter, I seek to retain the idea of system-change and futures that transcend capitalism. In particular, I focus on the scope for changing the place and role of work in society. I show how work can (and should) be transformed from a burden into a source of intrinsic reward, but I argue that such a transformation will require a fundamental shift in the way that work is performed. It will also require reducing work time and creating conditions where work fulfils real needs, as opposed to the demands of profit creation. Reimagining work, in short, will require a move to a post-capitalist system, in which human well-being and freedom are put at the centre of economic organization. Here I return to the writings of Marx and Morris, drawing on and applying their ideas about how the meaning of work might be changed under alternative socio-economic conditions.

The limits to growth

Modern economies focus on delivering a key objective, namely higher economic growth. More directly, they focus on increasing gross domestic product (GDP), which represents the monetary value of goods and services produced in the economy. Politicians promise increases in GDP as a way to win votes, while the public are presented with statistics on GDP and are asked to accept the idea that higher GDP is important and necessary for progress. An underlying idea is that higher economic growth is associated with higher employment and higher consumption and that people's lives will be improved by working and consuming in a growing economy. Economic policy fosters and perpetuates an ideology that 'growth is good' and is driven by a desire to expand the economy, seemingly without end.

The concentration on economic growth in policy-making reflects the influence of economics. The latter gives support and credence to a pro-growth approach. Economists, through their influence on policy and the media, have also created a wider public understanding of the need for economic growth. News outlets report GDP figures as if they are definitive guides to how the economy is going for ordinary people. GDP has become an accepted discourse for talking about the economy, even while it remains an abstract entity in its own right.[1]

Yet, in many respects, the benefits of economic growth for human well-being are debatable. Growth in GDP need not benefit all in society – indeed, it may come at the expense of a decline in the quality of people's lives. GDP cannot tell us how well people's lives are going because it is a measure of material output. It lacks the ability to uncover the qualitative conditions that define and shape the lives that people are actually able to lead.

The flaws in the growth of GDP as a goal of economic policy have been known by economists for years, but have tended to be pushed to one side.[2] At least up until recently, the flaws have not been thought important enough to think 'beyond GDP'. They include the neglect of the environmental damage done by economic growth. Economics refers to the external costs of economic growth, one of which is pollution. Another flaw (recognized by most economists) is GDP's failure to capture the value and importance of unpaid work, particularly that done in the act of caring for others. Feminist scholars have long argued that GDP statistics ignore the role and contribution of domestic labour done largely by women in society.[3]

For the purposes of this book, a further, more specific criticism can be added – that is, the inattention of GDP to the conditions and quality of work. GDP is not net of the costs of work that are incurred in producing valuable output. Rather, it ignores these costs. Work may decline in quality, but if GDP rises, the conclusion drawn is that the economy is advancing and that, by implication, well-being is improving. Yet this overlooks how the costs from work may be significant and how people's lives may be thwarted by work that is stultifying or alienating. Adam Smith, as we saw in chapters 2 and 5, recognized that higher economic growth would add to the costs of work – he worried, in particular, about the negative impacts of repetitive and simple work on workers' intelligence. But, again as discussed above, Smith saw these costs as inevitable. He refused to accept that the loss of workers' intelligence was a valid reason for forgoing economic growth – to the contrary, he argued that economic growth should be accelerated to offset the human costs of work. In this respect, he set the platform for future generations of economists to privilege the consumption benefits of work over its intrinsic costs.

The measurement and use of GDP also miss the advantages of expanding leisure time. Indeed, the increase in leisure time is seen as anathema to economic growth. Rather than seek more freedom from work, the imperative to increase economic growth translates into a case for expanding work for wages. There is no direct consideration within the economics of GDP of the specific goal and need to reduce work time.

One response here is to say that GDP is now being challenged from within economics. For example, the influential 'science of happiness' aims to dethrone GDP as an objective of economic policy.[4] Researchers (including many economists) have shown how there is no direct association between higher GDP levels and higher levels of reported happiness in advanced capitalist economies. Years of economic growth since the 1970s, it seems, have not made people in these economies any happier – rather, higher economic growth has left them feeling no better-off. This finding has fuelled calls for policy-makers to target increased happiness levels instead of higher economic growth.[5]

I am sympathetic to the criticisms made by happiness researchers. Their arguments that there are limits to economic growth – as far as human well-being is concerned – are important and timely. But I also have concerns with happiness research. Its focus on subjective well-being is particularly problematic. The failure to see how people can adapt to circumstances and report feeling happy in situations of adversity is a real problem. Reports of happiness may conceal the fact that people are not achieving well-being and there is an urgent need for progress in the conditions of life.[6]

As was shown in chapter 4, there are important objective dimensions to the quality of work that are at risk of being ignored if the focus is on how people feel about the work they do. Indeed, through the effects of adaptation, workers may report feeling satisfied in jobs that are objectively bad, highlighting the dangers of relying solely on subjective reports of well-being in assessing the quality of work. This illustrates the more general problem of using reports of subjective well-being to assess how well people's lives are going.

The other problem is that reported happiness is elevated as another goal to be maximized. Happiness replaces GDP. As argued above, there are problems with reported happiness as a measure of well-being. But there remains the argument that happiness can be maximized by growing the economy. New empirical evidence is invited to show how higher economic growth and higher reported happiness can be reconciled. Indeed, much debate has centred on whether happiness and economic growth are, in fact, positively related.[7] This debate has the potential to challenge the parameters of current policy, but at the same time, it limits the room for criticism. In particular, it fails to see how – beyond the pursuit of happiness or economic growth – there is a need to rethink the way work and life are organized in society. It is not a matter of generating more empirical evidence, but of developing the ideas and vision to conceive of a different future beyond the present.

In summary, the flaws of GDP are too important to ignore. A major problem is that GDP seeks to support, as oppose to change, capitalism. It supports people continuing in jobs even when these jobs may deny them the freedom to be creative and to have more free time. Again, while alternatives such as happiness research create some pressure for reform, the need remains for new thinking that goes beyond this research. The problem, in short, is not just that GDP growth does not make people happy, but that it reflects a system that is inimical to human well-being. Abandoning GDP ultimately means moving beyond capitalism itself.

Crisis capitalism

The paradox, of course, is that, for all the policy focus on raising GDP, capitalism has proved unable to achieve economic growth consistently. Instead, it has faced recurrent crises. These have brought higher unemployment and caused significant economic hardship. They have also demonstrated the need for change, not least in a direction that creates the basis for greater stability.

The period since the 1970s has witnessed a series of severe crises. While these have differed in their length and depth, they can be linked to particular circumstances within capitalist economies.[8] These circumstances include changes in policy, particularly the deregulation of labour and financial markets. They also link to wider shifts in the economy, including in prevailing power relations.[9] These shifts have come at the cost of higher inequality together with more sporadic and often anaemic economic growth.

Yet, despite this fact, each new crisis has witnessed a resolve to reproduce the status quo as opposed to change it. The global financial crisis that began in 2007–8 initially brought about some critical reflection on the future of the economy (and capitalism). This reflection, however, hardly lasted – indeed, it turned to an embrace of policies aimed at consolidating existing inequalities. Policy-makers looked to austerity to aid recovery – where 'recovery' meant workers sacrificing their incomes and life-chances in order to sustain the prosperity of those at the top of society. In truth, the aftermath of the 2007–8 crisis simply exposed the depth of the divisions that existed in society and the poverty of policy responses to crisis within capitalism. While austerity was resisted, its dominance helped to shape the contours of debate, to the point where it was difficult to see a future beyond it. In this process, resistance was kept within limits and ultimately quelled.

The COVID-19 crisis has been on a different scale from previous crises. In its initial stages, it led to a lockdown in the economy. In effect, the economy had to be curtailed to save lives. As it became dangerous for people to work together, so moves towards homeworking had to take place. Where homeworking was not possible, work had to be suspended, with workers sometimes paid not to work (hence, the rise in forms of furloughing). The continuation of the crisis at the time of writing has led to higher unemployment together with enforced reductions in work hours, with problems of underemployment.

At one level, the pandemic has offered a glimpse into what life might be like with a reduced work commitment. While some workers have found the adjustment to homeworking a struggle, others have experienced greater flexibility and freedom in the uses of their time. The pandemic has also offered a reminder of the importance of certain kinds of work – not least the work carried out by so-called 'key workers' in sectors such as health and retail. It has shown how the economy might be curtailed and refocused on need as opposed to profitability. Yet, at another level, the pandemic has highlighted society's collective dependency on work and the pressure that most people face to work for a living. Beyond the discussion about living with less work and the talk of key workers, there has been an inexorable drive and imperative to maintain the conditions of wage-labour and to restore business as usual.

There are, of course, debates about what a return to 'normality' – beyond COVID-19 – might look like. Does the future of work entail more homeworking, for example? Responses to the crisis – including state-supported job retention schemes – have brought into sharper focus the fragilities of the economy and the scope for a greater role for the state in ensuring economic and social stability. This is all to the good. But the risk, as in the past, is that any change will be temporary. Celebration of the efforts of key workers, for example, may be quickly replaced with deep cuts to budgets that limit pay rises and the increase in jobs in the public sector. The concern that national governments will reimpose austerity to 'balance the books' remains serious. Indeed, without any shift in prevailing political and economic doctrine, the return to austerity may seem inevitable. Beyond that, it is hard to see any move at a policy level to displace the same dominant growth model – the one based on the increase in inequality, which led to previous crises and made national economies (inclusive of their health and care systems) more vulnerable to the damage wrought by COVID-19.

Crisis capitalism has proved itself inadequate to the task of elevating the lives of the many in society. It has created unemployment for some and low-quality jobs for others. Where it has provided consumption, it has often been at the cost of rising levels of household debt.[10] While the latest crisis linked to COVID-19 may not have its origins within the capitalist system, it has shown the weaknesses of capitalism as a system designed to satisfy our needs. It is clear that a post-crisis imagination (and future) requires thinking that transcends the limits of the present.

Beyond full employment

One issue to confront in seeking a better future is that of full employment. Critical voices have argued for full employment against those (including many economists) who have justified unemployment as a mechanism for securing low inflation. Keynesian policies, in particular, centre on achieving full employment by manipulating aggregate demand. These policies link to the pursuit of higher economic growth, albeit in a way that supplies enough jobs for everyone to have work in society. A progressive capitalism is seen as one where work is plentiful and no one faces unemployment.

Full employment has not been a priority of national governments in the last few decades – rather, low and stable inflation has become the key goal, with national governments allocating responsibility for achieving this goal to independent central banks. Unemployment has also been addressed less by demand stimulus than by reform in labour markets – a tactic that has coincided with a retrenchment of the welfare state and the move away from a proper social safety net. National governments have eschewed Keynesian economics in favour of a market-based economics.

I make two points in relation to the goal of full employment. These points reveal some of the limitations of full employment as a long-term policy goal and the need to rethink policy and politics beyond it.

The first point relates to the understanding of Keynes's own vision of a better future. Properly understood, this vision did not equate to the creation of perpetually high levels of employment, but rather offered support for the move to 'full unemployment'. Keynes, as we saw in chapter 3, believed that the restoration of full employment was vital in achieving shorter work hours. Workers could only be assured of working less if they were empowered by full employment together with strong trade unions. But full employment represented an intermediate goal – beyond it, the ultimate goal was to reduce work time and release people from the strictures of work. Equating Keynes's policy doctrine with the constant pursuit of full employment misses how he imagined a better future where society would have less work to do – where work would cease to define human life. Following this line, any modern Keynesian policies, while focused on resolving unemployment, should also aim to reduce work time. The point is not to accept work's persistence, but to seek a future where its dominance and hold over people's lives are curtailed significantly. This means committing to work time reduction and the quest for a future based on greater free time.[11]

The second point concerns the political constraints on full employment. Keynes argued that capitalism needed to accommodate certain reforms – in particular, there was a need to create conditions where capital and labour could share in the benefits of productivity growth. Such conditions would be realized by pursuing full employment. But Keynes underestimated how capitalist employers would resist full employment as well as a more equitable distribution of income and how this resistance could prevent the realization of the positive future he outlined in his 1930 essay.

Keynes's contemporary Michał Kalecki wrote an article in 1943 that highlighted the political obstacles to full employment under capitalism. Capitalist employers, Kalecki argued, favoured unemployment as a means to maintain discipline at work. The threat of 'the sack' was made effective by the presence of unemployment, and capitalist employers' reliance on this threat meant that policies to achieve full employment would be blocked in practice. Even though capitalist employers could benefit from higher profits through the move to full employment, they would still resist such a move due to the destabilizing effects of lower unemployment on the balance of power in the workplace. Kalecki stressed the political pressures in society that would prevent policy-makers from enacting full employment policies. In this respect, he revived Marx's notion of the 'reserve army' of labour as a permanent feature of capitalist economies.

While the economic context may have changed since the time Kalecki wrote his article, the basis of his argument still stands, namely that capitalist employers have interests in maintaining unemployment rather than allowing policy-makers to resolve it. Discipline in the offices of twenty-first-century capitalism still requires some element of threat, whether directly via unemployed workers ready to replace incumbent workers, or indirectly through the use of workers on precarious contracts that can substitute for workers in permanent posts.

Kalecki argued that capitalism would have to undergo 'fundamental reform' to achieve full employment.[12] Capitalism had to evolve a different system of work – one based not on discipline and coercion but on cooperation and trust. The capacity of modern capitalism, given its deep economic and social divides, to accommodate such a system can be considered to be limited. At least, with the decline of trade unions and collective bargaining institutions, it is a long step from the present to a reformed capitalism capable of providing work for all.

The point is that the achievement of full employment entails confronting and overcoming issues of unequal power. Keynes's ideas helped to forge the kind of social democracy in the post-war period that accommodated class interests and set the basis for full employment. But, in the years since the 1970s, capitalism has been reformed in a regressive direction. The political constraints on full employment have become more evident and real. Any positive change will require, as emphasized by Kalecki, fundamental reform in society.

A further point can be added here. This relates to the potential trade-off between the volume and quality of work. As I noted in chapter 4, research showing the costs of unemployment can lead to policy recommendations that aim to create more work, even if the latter is low-quality. Keynes, for his part, highlighted the potential role of 'make-work' schemes in creating employment for people – half-jokingly, he referred to workers being paid by the state to bury bottles filled with money in the ground. Private enterprise could then be incentivized to dig them up. This scheme could help to boost aggregate demand and eliminate unemployment. But hole-digging was only to be contemplated if other, more worthwhile sources of employment could not be found.[13] Keynes was not in favour of pursuing work for its own sake. Further, for him, there was the long-term need to limit work rather than expand it. Work was not to be elevated above leisure but rather was to be reduced in order to expand people's freedom to pursue activities of their own choosing. Keynes's 1930 essay made this argument effectively.

In the present, higher levels of employment have often come at the expense of lower-quality work. Before the COVID-19 crisis, countries like the UK secured high levels of employment by creating more low-paid, insecure jobs. A 'jobs miracle' hid a chronic problem of low-quality work – a problem that has been linked directly to poor health outcomes.[14] The point is that full employment must be seen not just as a simple 'job count' but also as a measure of the quality of work that society is able to create.

Keynes and Kalecki may have differed on some matters of politics, but they were united in the belief that achieving full employment would require significant social and economic change. They also agreed on the need to challenge the constraints of work. Keynes had a vision of a future where work time would be curtailed – full employment was only a means to a higher goal, namely the reduction of work time and the increase in free time. Kalecki made a case for reforming work in a more democratic direction – pursuing full employment meant challenging the capitalist authority relation and injecting democracy into the workplace. The broader issue is that both writers did not limit their imagination to maximizing paid work, but instead contemplated the need for a future where workers would enjoy more freedom and autonomy over their work.

Full employment remains vital if workers are to secure cuts in work hours and improvements in the quality of work. But, as I have argued above, it must be seen as a stepping stone to a better world, one where the opportunity for people to live without work is extended and where work itself enhances human life. Goals beyond full employment must guide the reform of society.

As I will show in the next section, one important policy intervention designed to reduce people's dependency on paid work is a UBI. This policy is seen as a direct alternative to full employment and is proposed by some as a mechanism for creating a post-work future – one seemingly in tune with the prediction of Keynes's 1930 essay.

Income support

A UBI – an income payable to all citizens regardless of need and status – has been advocated for many years. It has gained prominence and support in recent years, thanks in part to concern with the potential problem of the loss of paid work through automation (see the discussion in chapter 6). Hence, in a world where jobs are set to run out, a UBI becomes a compelling and necessary option. A UBI has also been suggested as an emergency response to crisis and as a way to shore up the economy in the context of weak or falling aggregate demand.[15]

Interestingly, a UBI has received support at either end of the political spectrum. For those on the right, a UBI offers a way to empower people in markets and to reduce state bureaucracy. Milton Friedman, famously, advocated a 'negative income tax'.[16] The latter offers a cash payment to those who receive income below a certain threshold. In this way, it provides a supplement to income from paid work and a means to support the income of low earners. Friedman's interest in a UBI stemmed from a concern to extend the freedom of individuals and was consistent with his wider advocacy of a free-market capitalism. In the present, some prominent figures in business (including Elon Musk) have supported a UBI. Their concern has been to support consumption levels.[17] The reproduction of the economy has taken priority over the pursuit of other goals such as the reduction of work time.

On the left, by contrast, a UBI has been seen as part of a broader strategy to create greater freedom from work. Set at a generous level, a UBI would enable people to cut their hours of work and to enjoy more leisure time. Workers would not be forced to take low-quality work, but instead would be able to hold out for better work – a UBI would allow for improvements in the quality of work. But a UBI would pose a more direct challenge to wage-labour (and indeed to work itself). Specifically, it would give people the freedom to indulge their passions in all manner of creative activities outside of work. Some critics of work see a UBI as a key foundation for a post-work society in which the dominance of work is vanquished and free time is extended to all.[18]

I think a UBI has certain advantages. In particular, it offers a means to decouple income from work. In this sense, it provides the potential to strengthen worker bargaining power in labour markets, facilitating progress in wages and working conditions. It also offers a way to rethink life beyond the constant pursuit of work and money – indeed, it creates space for more leisure-centred ways of living that transcend work for wages. But I believe it also presents some difficulties. Firstly, by its nature and design, it can easily be co-opted to support capitalism, not subvert it. A UBI, if introduced alongside cuts in the welfare state and withdrawal of benefits, may simply act as a subsidy to low-paid work. The claim that a UBI would be emancipatory, therefore, ignores how it can be implemented under capitalism and used to maintain capital accumulation and economic growth.[19]

Secondly, a UBI has a somewhat limited goal: it seeks to offer income for people to live with a reduced work commitment. It overlooks how people have other needs and goals, inclusive of work that they find meaningful and enjoyable. As mentioned above, it has been suggested that a UBI will empower workers in labour markets, enabling them to choose the jobs they desire. But this implies a continuation of wage-labour, with workers making more effective choices in existing labour markets. It also misses how change might be required in work not just to combat exploitation, but also to improve the quality of work. The issue of work reform remains a relative blind spot in discussions about a UBI.

This last point is important because even if we assume a UBI could be paid at a high level there would remain work for people to do. There would still be work required to create the surpluses for people to enjoy a UBI. The content of the work needed to pay everyone a UBI would then become a matter of critical scrutiny. There would be likely still to be some work that is low-quality. In this case, there would remain ethical concerns about the quality of work that would require interventions beyond a UBI.[20]

My point is not that a UBI would be undesirable or unworkable, but that it would offer only limited scope for changing work in society. I make this point with an awareness of how the idea and goal of a UBI have been presented as something like a panacea for the ills of society.[21] A UBI does challenge capitalism to some degree, but it also risks becoming a means to support it. It also neglects questions about the value of work. Indeed, at worst, it could prevent people from enjoying the rewards that work can bring. I would suggest that real change in work will only come about with wider reforms that are unrelated to a UBI. As I will argue below, one important reform is that of reduced work time, and more directly, the move to a four-day work week.

Working less is more

The idea of curtailing work hours, as we saw in chapter 3, draws support from different angles. One line of argument justifies shorter hours of work as a way to break the work-centred culture of society. Extending people's freedom to live as they want means shortening the time they spend at work. This emphasizes the costs of work and benefits of leisure. Another argument sees reduced work hours as a way to share work, not just to combat problems such as unemployment and underemployment, but also to challenge existing bases of gender inequality. Feminist perspectives argue for shorter work hours as a way to equalize the distribution of paid and unpaid work in society. A move to shorter work hours would also allow for more community engagement and greater participation in politics. Finally, from an ecological standpoint, reduced work hours can help with mitigating the effects of climate change. By shortening work hours, production and consumption could be reduced, alleviating pressure on the natural environment.

All these arguments have merit and are supported here. I also stressed in chapter 3 how reducing work time could potentially add to the quality of work, both by reducing exposure to bad work and by extending the opportunity for high-quality work. Working less, in short, is not just about escaping work but also about securing better work.

I propose, as a key goal of society, the curtailment of working time. I argue, in particular, that society should aim for a working week that is four days in length.[22] This aim would reflect a commitment to lessen the hold of work over human life. It would mean ensuring that work is shared out and that access to free time is equalized – some people (the unemployed and underemployed) would work more, while others (those in full-time work) would work less. As argued above, beyond facilitating the reduction of unemployment and underemployment, a four-day work week would help to promote goals of gender equality and ecological sustainability. It would also provide the basis for improvements in the quality of work, if accompanied by changes in how work is conducted.

I realize that the move to a four-day work week will require shifts in policy and politics. Specifically, it will require that the state enact policies to allow workers to work fewer hours. At present, workers are constrained in their ability to work less, in particular, by employers' power to set work hours. Many workers, in practice, lack the bargaining power to work fewer hours and face cuts in pay in the event of their taking part-time work (if such work exists). It is evident that the state could play a role in rebalancing power towards workers, enabling the latter to secure shorter work hours with no necessary loss in pay.

At a practical level, there is a role for new legal restrictions on work time. The state, for example, could set a target of a four-day work week in the economy and commit via changes in the law to realize this target. Legal changes here could include imposing an upper limit on the working work – one that could be adjusted downwards in line with productivity growth and agreed through negotiation with employers and trade unions. The gradual move to a shorter working week could be enshrined in law and made a part of sector-level agreements (with possible variation by sector to allow time for adjustment to a new, lower average working week).[23] But legal limits here would remain important in establishing a framework and momentum for change. Such limits might also encompass legal protections that enable workers to disconnect from work and to avoid the need to write and reply to electronic messages relating to work. This would help to protect leisure from the encroachment of work.[24]

In some countries, there already exist legal limits on working time. The European Working Time Directive (EWTD), for example, sets an upper limit of forty-eight hours on the working week, though some EU countries have 'opt-outs' that raise issues over its effectiveness. In addition, the EWTD has not undergone any major revisions for several decades, in part due to opposition from national governments. An important step would be to adopt a lower upper limit on the working week – hence, instead of a limit of forty-eight hours per week, a limit could be set at thirty-eight hours, at least initially. This could become a legal basis for a more general cut in weekly work hours across EU countries. To ensure compliance, opt-out clauses could also be phased out. More widely, a new and revised EWTD could set a target of an average working week of thirty hours by some future point, say in 2050 – this could be allied with an EU-wide, legally enforced 'right to disconnect'. For countries outside the EU, including the UK, the goal would be to adopt a similar target, based on new legislation.

In enacting policy, the state could take the lead in adopting a four-day work week within the public sector, and could look to apply pressure on the private sector to cut work hours via the procurement contracts it signs with private firms.[25] Tax incentives could also be used to encourage firms to reduce work hours without eroding wages. In addition, new entitlements to leave (for care and other responsibilities) could be implemented, alongside lowering the retirement age. Beyond these measures, the state could create new forums for social dialogue on the scope for a reduction in work time – a new Working Time Commission, for example, could be instituted to review and revise existing laws on working time and to monitor and assess progress towards work time reduction.[26] By bringing social partners together, such an initiative would help to build consensus and the basis for collective action and reform.

Trade unions, in particular, would have a significant role to play in bringing about change. History shows that unions have led the way in reducing work hours. Restoring unions' ability to enrol members and to organize would help to facilitate progress towards shorter work hours. It would be important that trade unions take the lead in focusing on work time reduction, including that goal as part of a broader demand for a more sustainable way of working.[27] In countries such as the UK and US, where collective bargaining and union power have been eroded, there would be a need for new support from the state to promote trade unions' role and influence. The goal here, again, would be to create the collective alliances and pressure required to curtail work time.

It must be acknowledged that concerns over income (and its potential reduction) hold back many households from reducing their work hours. This constraint is magnified by high levels of debt and the high cost of living (e.g. linked to housing), which drive the need for workers to keep working long hours. Inequality of income also underpins competitive consumption and perpetuates long work hours (see the discussion in chapter 3). Therefore, other policy measures will be needed. For example, there will be a need for higher progressive taxes (on wealth and income) and for wider policies of redistribution to raise the income of low earners. Policies that tackle consumerism will also have to be reviewed – for instance, curbs on advertising could be used to reduce the pressure to consume.[28]

The wider goal of all these policies would be to create conditions where a four-day work week is achievable for all. Policy intervention would be driven by a concern to level the playing field and provide the power and opportunity for workers to work less. Evidence showing workers cannot achieve the work hours they desire justifies action. Further, the fact that there remains evidence of national economies achieving shorter work hours without harm to living standards reinforces the case for change. Countries like Germany and the Netherlands, with shorter working weeks and relatively high living standards, show what is feasible. But it is evident that more deep-rooted reforms – led by the state and forged through new social partnerships – will be needed if modern societies are ever to realize the benefits of a four-day work week. In the next section, I outline further reforms – beyond the regulation of work time – that would yield progress in the quality of work.

Reimagining work

The argument I make here is a radical one – one that seeks to rethink the role and functions of work in life. Work is usually regarded as an activity that is undertaken for monetary ends. I suggest – against this way of thinking – that work be re-established as an activity aimed at meeting human needs, as opposed to monetary goals. I propose reforms in the way that work is directed, organized and governed. Such reforms demand that the economy as a whole is rethought and restructured.

Fundamentally, to identify the problem of work, we must examine issues of power and control. Work is a burden under capitalism because workers have no direct say over how it is done and the goals it seeks to fulfil. The sense of alienation linked to work has a real basis in workers' lack of power to control and direct the work they do. Marx's notion of alienating work retains relevance and resonance. It shows effectively how the resistance to work is connected not to the nature of work itself, but to the social relations that characterize capitalism. Work resistance is a systemic problem, not one linked to contingencies in the workplace.

From a reform perspective, then, power in society has to shift, from capital owners to workers, if work is to be changed. The goal should be to make workers owners of the workplaces in which they work and directors and controllers of the work they do. Beyond that, society needs to create conditions where workers value work because it means something to them and contributes to their well-being.

Reforms here include creating the conditions for greater worker ownership of firms. Backing for reforms like a UBI, as mentioned above, can slide into support for capitalism.

A four-day work week, likewise, may become a means for capitalist firms to be seen as more ethical and sustainable when their underlying work practices remain unchanged. Some capitalist firms, for example, may require workers to work more in fewer work hours, undermining any benefit for workers of a shorter working week. My point here is that worker ownership provides more of a challenge to capitalist firms. In particular, it challenges the rights of managers to manage and of owners to acquire the surpluses generated in work. It creates the basis for a more radical politics of work – one where workers are seen more as equals and joint owners, rather than as subordinates and hired hands to be treated as disposable assets.

I suggest two ways in which worker ownership could be encouraged. Here I focus on the role of the state and distinguish between policies that aim at changes in ownership under capitalism and those aimed at effecting broader changes in the economy beyond capitalism. In the second case, I see the basis for creating a different economy where economic democracy replaces capitalist rule in and over work.

Firstly, in practical terms, worker ownership implies state support for measures such as profit-sharing schemes and obligatory participation of workers on company boards. It also means support for stronger unions and for employee buyouts. In times of crisis, as in the COVID-19 pandemic, the state can use grants and loans to shift ownership. The state, for example, could take equity stakes in private firms and use the leverage it gains through ownership to ensure that workers share in profits and are involved in decision-making functions. Crisis can become an opportunity to democratize work.[29] In the case of the COVID-19 crisis, however, this opportunity has not been taken – a fact that highlights the barriers to reform. More directly, the state could facilitate the formation of worker-owned firms – for instance, by offering favourable loans and training in finance and management to would-be worker owners. Obviously, these reforms might be resisted by capital owners, but they can be seen as necessary to support wider changes in firm ownership and governance. Indeed, their enactment can be viewed as vital in creating the conditions for progress in the quality of work and life.[30]

Secondly, beyond the above reforms, there is a need for the state to own broader parts of the economy. What I envision here is the move to an economy that is more democratic and equalitarian in nature – one that aims to provide vital goods and services more on the basis of need than on the ability to pay. The agenda for change would entail rolling back the privatization programmes of the past and pushing forward the frontiers of the state. It would emulate the success of post-war Western capitalist economies in curbing high unemployment and high economic inequality, but would also seek to build a new social contract based on the sharing of economic surpluses and the promotion of higher well-being.

Importantly, work may be expanded under this agenda, but in areas where there is seen to be a real need, from education and health through to utilities such as water and transport. Again, one insight gained from the COVID-19 crisis has been the essential nature of some work, notably that carried out by workers in the public sector. Expansion of the public sector, with more workers trained and hired to provide vital public services, can be seen as consistent with ensuring that society functions in a healthy and sustainable way. Public sector expansion could go hand in hand with moves to curtail work time. A four-day work week, indeed, may require hiring more workers to maintain continuity in service, but then this extra hiring can be seen as justified to meet wider goals, including shorter work hours. The vision here is of an expanded public sector coinciding with a four-day work week.

Further, with the state taking a greater role in the economy, room can be made for initiatives such as a Green New Deal.[31] The state, for example, could aim to boost employment in retrofitting houses to reduce energy usage

and emissions. It could also seek to hire workers directly
to help in schemes such as coastal management and protection, plus rewilding the countryside.[32] Further, the state
could lead in investing in new technology that aims at
carbon reduction – generally, as others have argued, the
state could look to manage the process of innovation and
investment by setting ambitious 'missions' that prioritize a
future where the work done in society meets wider social
and economic goals.[33] The important point is that work
may be created and even guaranteed by the state.

Some modern writers have called for a 'job guarantee'.
This is partly motivated by a desire to reduce unemployment, but it has also been linked to the reduction of work
hours.[34] If workers are guaranteed work, their bargaining
power will be increased and they can secure cuts in work
hours. I support a job guarantee where it allies with an
attempt to channel work in the direction of need, but resist
it as an effort simply to create work for people to do. The
goal of a job guarantee must be to provide work that is
needed and valued by society and that, from workers' perspective, yields meaningful activity. It should not impose
work on low pay and in made-up tasks.[35]

The broader aim of these reforms would be to create a
situation where – using Morris's language – 'useless toil'
is replaced by 'useful work'. Under capitalism, as Morris
stressed, the waste of human efforts and talents as well as
the destruction of the natural environment arise from the
persistence of work that is linked to profit creation. By
reorientating work to more social and ethical aims, this
waste and this destruction could be eliminated – indeed,
human efforts and talents together with the natural
environment could be nurtured in ways that make life
better and worth living. Rethinking work in these ways,
in short, suggests creating an economy that is in harmony
with human and planetary needs. It also suggests creating
work that people find meaningful and enjoy doing – 'useful
work', then, may be expected to add to the well-being of
those performing it.

Other reforms would be needed to improve the quality of work. Firstly, following the discussion in chapter 6, technology would have to be harnessed in ways that deliver not just shorter work hours but also better work. Automation, under worker ownership, would help to minimize the drudgery of work and extend the opportunity for pleasure in work. Secondly, there would be a need to ensure some variety in work, allowing workers to rotate tasks, rather than be tied to any one task. This would be important, in particular, where non-automatable work survived that was costly for workers to perform. Rotation of tasks could also help to challenge gender norms and promote greater equity in the balance of work across genders. Thirdly, it would be important to reimagine the workplaces in which work is carried out. They should not only be safe and healthy places to work, but also sites of creativity and bases for solidarity and comradeship. If workers become owners, then work can be designed to facilitate creating great work alongside protecting the environment. Cooperative work, in the end, should be undertaken in ways that enable individual development, strengthen social ties and meet sustainability goals.

To summarize, my argument is not that work should be eliminated through reform. This is the mistaken argument made in some versions of post-work politics. Rather, it is that human life can be improved by work and that a key objective of reform is to reinstate work as a positive and life-improving activity. In line with both Marx and Morris, I promote the idea of a post-capitalist future, based on its potential to give people the opportunity to enjoy work as a part of their lives. In Morris's terms, 'joyless labour' under present-day capitalism must be replaced by 'work as art' in the future.[36] The enjoyment of work would be matched by the enjoyment of leisure, and pleasurable work would provide a foundation for a rewarding life in general.

In envisioning such change, I recognize the constraints imposed by existing ownership relations. Capitalist firms will not wane in influence without the pressure of a reforming state together with the collective force of trade unions, workers, activists and concerned citizens. The reforms I have put forward will be resisted and hence will take effort and time to promote. But such resistance only underlines the need to press for their realization. The vision of a better future of work must be invoked in the push for – and achievement of – a fundamentally different society.

8
Conclusion

Nature will not be finally conquered till our work becomes
a part of the pleasures of our lives.

William Morris, 'Useful Work
versus Useless Toil' (1884)

Making light work

The position I have taken in this book has two key elements. Firstly, I have stressed that work can be – and often is – a burden and a barrier to well-being. Past and present complaints about work are not made up or elaborate fictions, but instead have real meaning and reflect how work has been structured and imposed on people, to the detriment of their health and well-being. Injustices linked to work – including the persistence of unemployment and the presence of dehumanizing work conditions – highlight failures of the system that dominates in capitalist economies.

The second element is that there is a need for change in how work is conducted, not just to combat the costs of work itself, but also to make room for meaningful and pleasurable work. The idea that work can be enhanced in qualitative terms has motivated an agenda aimed at reforming work. It is not about seeking a future without work; rather, it is about creating the basis for a world where all the activities people undertake – whether in work or beyond it – are sources of meaning and pleasure. I have recognized that work will persist into the future and that moral and ethical questions will remain over how work is allocated and organized in society.

The lightening of work, in this context, has been shown to have a double meaning. Firstly, it means attempts to ease the burden of work. I have supported the case for reducing work time. Indeed, I have stressed the merits of realizing a four-day work week (and beyond that, potentially, a three-day work week). Keynes's vision of people in capitalist societies working fifteen hours per week stands as a world to be realized. Secondly, the lightening of work means securing the benefits of work. It means people having the opportunity to find meaning and pleasure in work and for them to contribute as producers to the shaping of a better society – one that is not only just and equitable, but also more sustainable and conducive to well-being.

I have argued that, in assessing the quality of work, there is a need to move beyond the notion of bullshit jobs – as presented by Graeber – and towards a conception that recognizes the objective barriers that workers face in achieving well-being in work. I have stressed, too, the scope to create greater opportunity for people to undertake work that is high-quality. Arguments from mainstream neoclassical economics and libertarian philosophy that justify, on freedom and efficiency grounds, the restriction of high-quality work in society have been exposed as false. Further, I have shown how the progress of technology – while often viewed in modern debate as a mechanism for reducing work – is likely to maintain work. Technological innovations may also lead more people to work in less rewarding jobs.

Finally, I have argued for a set of reforms that seek to challenge the system of work under capitalism. I have stressed how changes in ownership can facilitate wider reforms in work and how progress towards democracy in work can combine with injecting meaning and pleasure into work. Goals are needed that go beyond just guaranteeing income to people – rather, there is a need for policies and programmes that aim to reimagine work in a manner that adds to workers' freedom and well-being. I have emphasized the role of the state in facilitating structural change. Beyond that, I have promoted the vision of a future economy where work not only enables human development, but also meets goals of ecological sustainability and equality in society.

I can offer a brief sketch here of a future workplace where work is lightened. Such a workplace would be a venue for variety in work. Technology would be used, but in ways that protect and promote human skill and ingenuity – it would never degrade work, because that would contravene the goal of lightening work. In work, workers would take on tasks according to their abilities and would share out tasks that are irksome. There would be pressure to reduce work that is painful – indeed, there would be an insistence that such work is minimized in order to raise the average quality of work. There would also be democratic participation in work and the eschewal of hierarchy. Finally, there would be an attempt to provide ample opportunity for people to live lives beyond work and to create and produce in leisure. Indeed, the goal would be to blur the divide between work and leisure, so that enjoyment in life can be achieved in all spheres of human activity.

This ideal workplace would be situated in a transformed economy. The focus on work being undertaken for money-making would be replaced with an emphasis on working for the fulfilment of needs. This shift would imply some curtailment of work, as the pressure to accumulate and expand consumption would be diminished. But it would also imply some change in the nature of work. In the process of meeting needs through work, there would be an emphasis on making work more valuable in itself. The social purpose of work would be more obvious – objectively, work would not be pointless or bullshit, but rather would be about serving society. This fact would help to enhance the quality of work and would combine with reform in work to establish the basis for work that people enjoy doing.

The point is that a wider transformation in work would imply reform in its structures and organization. It would entail rethinking work beyond its limits under existing capitalist social relations. Again, automation (linked to new digital technologies) is unlikely to create any momentum for change, at least while it is restricted by the goals of capital accumulation. Decisive change will require shifting the focus of the economy towards needs-fulfilment and repurposing technology to facilitate more varied, interesting and lighter work.

Measures of progress, then, would not equate to raising economic growth or reported happiness levels (as signalled in surveys). Instead, they would entail assessing how well the economy furthers specific goals, from the elimination of want to the progress in reducing work time and expanding higher-quality work. They would also emphasize overcoming inequality linked to gender, and protecting the natural environment. The demand for work and an economy that serves people and the planet, in short, would underpin a broader commitment to elevate human values over capitalist imperatives.

I will add one further point. This concerns the limits of theory. I have shown how economics has exerted a particular influence on ideas about work, promoting a view of it as a means to income and linking it to increasing economic growth. Economics, too, has continued to influence ideas in the policy realm, supporting the maintenance of work and arguing that workers choose the work they do. Ideologically, economics has proved a barrier to collective reform aimed at promoting shorter work hours and higher-quality work. I suggest that economics needs to be challenged. New economic thinking, in particular, is needed to challenge the hegemony of mainstream neoclassical economics. But there is also a need for a renewal of political economy. More directly, there is a requirement for a political economy of work.

By political economy, I mean theory-building in the tradition of classical economics. While I have been critical of classical economists, I would take from their writings a history-centred view of the economy and a need to integrate ideas from across disciplines. The demise of classical economics in the latter part of the nineteenth century coincided with the eclipse of political economy in economics. Political economy was kept alive by Keynes, though against a background where neoclassical economics was attempting to formalize economics and turn it into a 'science', divorced from other social sciences. Political economy has survived in heterodox economics, but on the margins of economics debates and without real influence on mainstream opinion in either economics or policy circles.

A political economy approach would foreground the importance of work as a formative activity. It would stress the costs of work under capitalism – the lack of meaning in work would be linked directly to ideas of alienation. But it would also highlight the need to transform work. It would stress the idea and goal of negating alienating work and restoring a form of work that is rewarding in itself, in particular. Allied to this would be the commitment to realize futures beyond the present. Our economic imagination would expand to encompass alternative ways of working and living.

A revived political economy would fit with a restatement of Marx's and Morris's approaches. It would also open the way for new debate that does not just criticize the prevailing economics of work but also identifies reforms that could bring about change in how work is performed. Political economy can inspire a new politics aimed at securing both fewer work hours and an improved quality of work. One contribution of this book is to propose that a political economy of work be developed and used to promote change in – and beyond – the current system of work.

As mentioned in the introduction, the backdrop to this book is a crisis – indeed, the most serious crisis for capitalist economies in living memory. This crisis, of course, is the COVID-19 pandemic. It has upended the world of work. In addition to placing upward pressure on unemployment, the crisis has led to heavier workloads, and worse and often unsafe conditions of work. Shifts to homeworking have brought some flexibility for workers, but often at the expense of longer work hours together with new forms of remote monitoring.[1] Yet, at a deeper level, the crisis has exposed the long-standing inequalities in society, from undervalued and underpaid 'key workers' to the inadequacies of labour protections that leave all workers vulnerable to poor treatment at the hands of employers.

I am conscious that the COVID-19 crisis threatens to prevent the kind of reform agenda proposed in this book. It could do so directly by weakening workers' ability to fight for change. If higher unemployment occurs beyond the crisis, employers will be able to impose stricter conditions on workers, from longer work hours and higher work intensity to cuts in pay and erosions in non-wage benefits such as pensions. Any duty on the part of employers to protect jobs and livelihoods will quickly disappear if national governments withdraw their support for higher public spending and reimpose austerity policies. In this case, the legacy of COVID-19 will be a consolidation of the same inequalities that existed before the crisis struck.

But a reason for writing this book is to suggest that another path is possible and necessary. The focus should not be on restoring the old normal, but instead on creating a new normal. An important goal in rebuilding the economy, as argued above, should be to reform work, turning it from a burden into a source of meaning and pleasure.

Any reform agenda must be built on redistributing power and introducing democracy into work.

I take some hope, however, from the fact that the crisis has opened up new space for dissent and criticism. The barriers to change remain formidable. But the crisis is a powerful reminder of the present system's deficiencies. The likelihood is that, if and when the economy recovers and national governments reapply the economic policies of the past, capitalist economies will face yet another crisis – one linked to errant economic policies rather than to a pandemic. The hope, though, is that, against the odds, pressure for change will mount and lead to the kind of collective action that is needed to reform society.

I see other sources of hope. Firstly, there is the recent rise in unionization. The formation of new unions in the gig economy is a particularly welcome development.[2] The labour movement in some countries (e.g. the UK) is also now looking to back progressive goals such as a four-day work week.[3] These developments bode well for creating the conditions for broader social change, at least if matched with political parties that wish to make such change possible.

Secondly, there is the rise of think tanks and campaigning groups promoting the cause for change in the way that work is conducted. Noteworthy are the campaigns for a four-day work week that have sprung up in Europe.[4] These have helped to influence policy debate directly.[5] Momentum for change has been fuelled by different books, including Graeber's. While I have been critical of post-work politics, I think it serves a useful purpose in opening the way for more critical debate on work, as it exists now and how it might exist in the future. The present book is an attempt to add to, and extend, this debate, with a view to galvanizing action for change.

Thirdly, there is the sense of hope that comes from weariness with the present. While powerful forces prevent change, things cannot go on as they are. Allied to this is the hope for something better. The crisis linked to COVID-19, again, has demonstrated how the present system is inadequate to meet our most basic needs. But it has also offered a window on a different future. Enforced homeworking has demonstrated the possibilities for granting workers greater autonomy over when and how they work. Restricting the economy to essential activities has demonstrated the pointlessness of some existing work and the scope to refocus the economy on fulfilling needs, as opposed to the demands of capital owners. Of course, as argued above, there are many who would like to return the economy to where it was before the crisis. But the cracks in the system are now more evident than before the crisis, and while policies and politics may paper over these cracks, they cannot prevent them from widening. The public might yet demand change and the move beyond the present system.

On this last point, let me stress the need to keep alive and develop ideas that promote and press for change. Here again I see particular merit in the writings of Marx and Morris. As I have stressed, their writings not only challenge and contest how many of us work and live in the present, but also fire our imaginations about a better future. Indeed, they demand that change be made to realize this future. To be sure, there is scope to develop these writings. But my argument is that they offer a base on which to rethink work and life. In particular, through engagement with and development of Marx's and Morris's ideas, it is possible to see a way to 'build back better' in a real, rather than just a rhetorical, sense.

I will end the book by refocusing on the notion of the lightening of work. This is not simply a description of what the world might be like, but also a demand for the transcendence of the world that exists now. Creating work that is not just shorter in duration but also a part of life is an important step in subverting existing reality. The notion of lightening work helps to develop a more critical awareness of what could and should be achieved in a post-crisis and post-capitalist future. This book is an attempt to show

how far society is from lightening work and what should be done to bring about lighter work in the future.

I have stressed here how, beyond rhetoric about mass automation and possible futures without work, there is a need for collective action to achieve progress in the quality of work. The key task is to ensure that work is transformed and that the economy comes to respect human needs for productive activity. Finding a balance between work and non-work activities means cutting hours of work, but it also means taking action to transform work itself. I have suggested that the vision of work transformation is compatible with wider goals of sustainability and equality in society and that realizing this vision necessitates moving beyond capitalism.

In conclusion, I hope this book helps to push forward debate on work, in its present and possible future forms. I hope, more directly, that it will spur greater critical thinking about work and that, in line with the contributions of Marx and Morris, it will spark thoughts (and actions) that aim to recreate work in the future. Above all, I hope that the book will leave the reader in no doubt that work can and must be lightened, for the benefit of all humanity.

Notes

1 Introduction

1 J. Chapelard, 'Plumber Who Won £14 Million Lottery Jackpot Back at Work Fixing Toilets Two Days Later', *Mirror*, 21 July 2016 (available at: https://www.mirror.co.uk/news/uk-news/plumber-who-won-14million-lottery-8462478).

2 Many lottery winners choose not to quit working, but rather to work fewer hours. The sense of work being something good in life and worth pursuing for its own sake seems to drive the decision to keep working. See, for example, the research findings reported in Picchio et al. (2018).

3 For historical studies of the concept and activity of work, see John Budd's *The Thought of Work* (Budd, 2011) and Andrea Komlosy's *Work* (Komlosy, 2018). For different critical accounts of work, see Edward Granter's *Critical Social Theory and the End of Work* (Granter, 2009), Kathi Weeks's *The Problem with Work* (Weeks, 2011), Peter Fleming's *The Mythology of Work* (Fleming, 2015), David Frayne's *The Refusal of Work* (Frayne, 2015), David Graeber's *Bullshit Jobs* (Graeber, 2018) and Josh Cohen's *Not Working* (Cohen, 2018).

4 See, for example, Nick Srnicek and Alex Williams, *Inventing*

the Future (Srnicek and Williams, 2015), Paul Mason, *Postcapitalism* (Mason, 2015) and Rutger Bregman, *Utopia for Realists* (Bregman, 2018).

5 See, for example, Erik Brynjolfsson and Andrew McAfee, *The Second Machine Age* (Brynjolfsson and McAfee, 2014), Martin Ford, *The Rise of the Robots* (Ford, 2015) and Daniel Susskind, *A World Without Work* (Susskind, 2020).

6 *The Political Economy of Work* (Spencer, 2009).

7 Marmot et al. (2020) discuss the uneven economic and social impacts of COVID-19 in the UK and propose a set of new reforms to 'build back better'.

8 On the 'build back better' agenda, see 'OECD Policy Responses to Coronavirus (COVID-19)', OECD, 5 June 2020 (available at: http://www.oecd.org/coronavirus/policy-responses/building-back-better-a-sustainable-resilient-recovery-after-covid-19-52b869f5).

2 Meanings of Work

1 For a discussion of early ideas on work, see Anthony (1977).

2 Genesis 3:19.

3 Locke (1706: 53).

4 Furniss (1920) provides the definitive study of mercantilist labour doctrine. The discussion that follows draws on his work.

5 Daniel Defoe, for example, pronounced that 'there's nothing more frequent, than for an Englishman to work till he has got his pocket full of money, and then go and be idle, or perhaps drunk, till, 'tis all gone' (Defoe, 1704: 27). See also Thomas (2009: 80–1).

6 The view was that workers would live 'better lives' if they were subject to constant work on low wages (Furniss, 1920: 121–2). See also Thomas (2009: 85, 90–1).

7 Thompson (1967) offers a detailed account of the patterns of work prior to capitalism and the tightening in the discipline of work that occurred in the move to capitalism.

8 Hatcher (1998: 115) and Thomas (2009: 109).

9 Coats (1958) and Hatcher (1998) discuss the move to a more 'liberal' attitude towards the position of the labourer in society within late eighteenth-century economic thought.

10 'Where wages are high', Smith (1976, vol. 1: 99) wrote, 'we shall always find the workmen more active, diligent, and expeditious, than when they are low.'

11 Smith offered a clear ethical argument for higher wages. He wrote emphatically that: 'No society can surely be flourishing and happy, of which the far greater part of the members are poor and miserable. It is but equity, besides, that they who feed, clothe, and lodge the whole body of the people, should have such a share of the produce of their own labour as to be themselves tolerably well fed, clothed, and lodged' (Smith, 1976, vol. 1: 96). Here he overturned the 'utility of poverty' thesis found in mercantilism (Martin, 2015).

12 Smith (1976, vol. 1: 99) identified a 'progressive state' with an economy where wages were rising and 'happiness' was growing. Progress in society, for him, meant securing the conditions for rapid economic growth. These conditions were best achieved by enforcing strong property rights and by allowing individuals the freedom to pursue their own interests.

13 With the focus on an 'optimal' wage, there remained some scepticism among the classical economists that wages could keep on rising – at least, there was some idea of an upper limit on wages that would be set by the need to deter idleness among workers (Coats, 1967: 111).

14 Smith (1976, vol. 1: 47).

15 Smith (1976, vol. 1: 116–17) developed the idea – later to form part of the economic theory of 'compensating differentials' – that wages will vary inversely with the quality of work (e.g. the most disagreeable jobs will command the highest wages). As discussed in chapter 5, this notion has been invoked to justify the non-regulation of labour markets and has come to be linked with a broader free-market ideology that favours individual choice over any kind of collective intervention initiated by the state or trade unions.

16 Smith (1976, vol. 2: 782).

17 The reference to homeopathy (or 'homeopathic doses' of education) derives from a critical comment made by Marx (1976: 484) against Smith.

18 Perelman (2010) addresses critically Smith's ideas on labour and their links to ideology.

19 Bentham (1983: 104; emphasis in original).

20 Malthus (1926: 358) wrote that: 'Necessity has been with great truth called the mother of invention.'

21 Mill (1984: 90).

22 Mill was highly critical of the way in which workers had become degraded by their work under industrial capitalism (see Mill, 1965: 756) – a line that led him to endorse radical reforms, from a slowing in economic growth to enable more leisure time (ibid.: 755–6) to the move to a cooperative mode of work organization based on worker ownership (ibid.: 792). Needless to say, his support for these reforms set him apart from other classical economists who favoured higher economic growth and the continuation of capitalism.

23 The economics of work – its nature and evolution – is covered in Spencer (2009). Spencer (2014) discusses the different meanings attached to the disutility of work in economics, both past and present.

24 Agency theory, as applied to the study of the workplace, focuses on the relationship between 'principals' (those who hire and manage workers) and 'agents' (those hired to work, i.e. workers). Formal models are built incorporating this relationship and are used on MBA programmes to educate current and would-be managers on how to manage the workplace (see, for example, Lazear and Shaw, 2007). The teaching of agency theory in business schools, in turn, has affected how managers think about the management process. For more on this effect and the potential harm it can do (and has done) to society, see Ferraro et al. (2005).

25 For criticisms of the application of agency theory to the analysis of work and the employment relationship, see Spencer (2013a).

26 See the many interviews in Terkel (1974), where workers convey effectively the burdens and deprivations of their daily work. See also the accounts in Graeber (2018), where numerous workers report the futility of the jobs they perform. I return to Graeber's account of 'bullshit jobs' in chapter 4.

27 Again, Thompson (1967) documents how work habits and disciplines changed in the move to capitalism.

28 Weber (1958: 182) referred pointedly to how the work ethic haunted 'our lives like the ghosts of dead religious beliefs'. I leave aside here the many criticisms of Weber's thesis and

instead focus on its ideational role in supporting a positive view of work.

29 In *Past and Present*, Carlyle (1843: 196) wrote that 'Labour is Life: from the inmost heart of the Worker rises his god-given Force, the sacred celestial Life-essence breathed into him by Almighty God; from his inmost heart awakens him to all nobleness, – to all knowledge, "self-knowledge" and much else, so soon as Work fitly begins.' Here he mixed religious rhetoric with ideas about the possibilities for self-development through work. He stressed how work should be pursued for goals beyond obtaining money and that work and life should exist in harmony. In all respects, he insisted that people work hard rather than idle away time.

30 See Carlyle (1849) for a defence of slavery, based on the alleged virtues of work.

31 Mill (1984: 90). See also note 22 above on Mill's ideas for work reform.

32 A study undertaken by Chandola and Zhang (2018) shows how the move from unemployment to low-quality employment can harm individual health and well-being. The costs of unemployment and of work are addressed in chapter 4.

33 Steve Jobs delivered a Commencement address, titled 'You've Got to Find what You Love', at Stanford University on 12 June 2005 (available at: https://news.stanford.edu/2005/06/14/jobs-061505). The line 'do what you love' has since been taken from the speech and used to promote a pro-work sentiment.

34 Tokumitsu (2015).

35 Marx (1973: 610).

36 Marx (1977: 68).

37 Marx (1977: 65).

38 Marx (1977: 66).

39 Marx (1976: 548).

40 Ibid.

41 Some Marxist writers have shown how consent to work can be manufactured in the workplace and how this consent can be a powerful factor in preventing change in work and beyond it. For a classic sociological study in this vein, see Burawoy (1979).

42 Morris (1993a: 367).

43 The view that all work was good, as Morris (1993b: 287)

put it, was 'a convenient belief to those who live on the labour of others'. It served their interests, at the expense of workers who suffered work as a pain.

44 A distinguishing characteristic of 'the working classes' was that they worked constantly and without 'hope of rest' (Morris, 1993b: 289). Capitalism simply prevented workers' freedom to pursue a life beyond work.

45 Morris (1993b: 289–92) offered a damning assessment of the capitalist class system, with a parasitical class of rich people at the top of society, a middle class producing very little but over-consuming via forms of competitive consumption, and the working classes (as 'the real producers') burdened by degrading work. The need to eliminate this system remained a key theme of his work.

46 Morris (1993b: 294) wrote contemptuously that capitalism did not produce 'real wealth', but instead contributed to 'the production of rubbish'.

47 Morris (1993b: 296) suggested that capitalism created 'joy-less labour' and reduced the life of workers to that of a 'hunted beast'.

48 In 'How We Live and How We Might Live', Morris (1979: 153) argued that the profit imperative fuelled pollution and ecological degradation: 'It is profit which draws men into enormous unmanageable aggregations called towns, for instance; profit which crowds them up when they are there into quarters without gardens or open spaces; profit which won't take the most ordinary precautions against wrapping a whole district in a cloud of sulphurous smoke; which turns beautiful rivers into filthy sewers, which condemns all but the rich to live in houses idiotically cramped and confined at the best, and at the worst in houses for whose wretchedness there is no name.'

49 See the discussion in 'The Hopes of Civilisation' (Morris, 1993c: 318). Here Morris showed how the progress of modern technology led to higher unemployment and less skilled work. Elsewhere, he (1993b: 304) mocked the notion of '"labour-saving" machines', showing how, in fact, tech-nological progress under capitalism added to the misery of work.

50 Thompson (1976) addresses the evolution of Morris's intel-lectual and political thought.

51 Morris (1993c: 327). Morris came to share Marx's view that capitalism would face recurrent crises and that the collective pressure of the working class would lead to the transition from capitalism to socialism.
52 Marx (1992: 959).
53 Marx (1972: 257; emphasis in original).
54 Marx (1975: 228; emphasis in original).
55 Marx and Engels (1976: 53).
56 The ideal society of the future would be based on principles of equality and equal contribution. In particular, everyone in society would contribute to productive activity and receive a living in return: 'All must work according to their ability, and so produce what they consume – that is, each man should work as well as he can for his own livelihood, and his livelihood should be assured to him; that is to say, all the advantages which society would provide for each and all of its members' (Morris, 1993b: 294).
57 Morris (1993b: 299) commented that the 'usefulness' of work could be 'counted on in sweetening tasks otherwise irksome'. Workers who performed useful work would gain a new appreciation and desire for work that would drive them to carry out the work itself. Following Marx, Morris also stated that reduced work hours would help to win workers' consent to work: 'much work which is now a torment, would be easily endurable if it were much shortened' (ibid.). Work performed over a shorter time period could then be more enjoyable as well as more productive.
58 Morris (1993d: 357, emphasis in original).
59 Morris (1993b: 305) suggested that society might arrange a scheme 'whereby those who did the roughest work should work for the shortest spells'. This would ensure that no one was restricted to the worst work all of the time and that there would be scope for people doing this work to do other, more attractive work. Again, the goal was to extend opportunities for pleasure in work.
60 As Morris (1993b: 305) put it, 'let us see if the heavens will fall on us if we leave it [bad work] undone, for it were better that they should. The produce of such labour cannot be worth the price of it.'
61 Morris (1993b: 299–300) supported the need for 'variety of work'. It was clear to him that the current education

system needed to be radically reformed if people were to be empowered to perform different tasks in work.

62 Morris (1993b: 301) discussed the requirement to create 'pleasant surroundings' at work – ones that would support workers' health and help to protect the natural environment.

63 Morris (1993b: 302) linked the move to socialism with superior environmental and social outcomes.

64 Weeks (2011: 13) and Frayne (2015: 8). These contributions build on earlier perspectives such as that of Gorz (1985).

65 Srnicek and Williams (2015).

66 Weeks (2011: 86–8).

67 Weeks (2011: 104–9) defends the focus on less work over better work. A particular concern is that the goal of better work has been adopted by human resource management and has been deradicalized as a result – indeed, it has become a justification for more work. The goal of less work, by contrast, retains a radicalism in rejecting work and should be given priority in the critique of work. I challenge this view in the discussion that follows.

68 Weeks (2011: 109) does admit at one point that: 'The struggle to improve the quality of work must be accompanied by efforts to reduce its quantity.' But this insight is obscured by an insistence that work be refused and rejected. Focus on the goal of less work crowds out consideration of the goal of better work. There is a lack of balance in post-work politics, and more directly, a lack of clarity on ways to reform and transform work beyond capitalism.

69 For a similar line of criticism, including an invocation of Morris on the different possible uses of technology and a defence of work activity from a Marxist standpoint, see Bellamy Foster (2017).

3 The (Lost) Dream of Working Less

1 M. Matouseke, 'Elon Musk Says You Need to Work at Least 80 Hours a Week to Change the World', *Business Insider*, 27 November 2018 (available at: https://www.businessinsider. com.au/elon-musk-says-80-hours-per-week-needed-change-the-world-2018-11).

2 E. Johnson, 'Full Q&A: Tesla and SpaceX CEO Elon

Musk on Recode Decode', *Vox*, 5 November 2018 (available at: https://www.vox.com/2018/11/2/18053428/recode-decode-full-podcast-transcript-elon-musk-tesla-spacex-boring-company-kara-swisher).

3 Keynes (1963).
4 Bienefeld (1972) and Pencavel (2018) discuss the role of organized labour in reducing work hours in the UK and the US. Hunnicutt (1988) examines the influence of the labour movement in the US on work time.
5 Keynes (1963: 368).
6 Keynes (1963: 366–7).
7 Keynes (1963: 371–2).
8 Matthew 6:28 contains the line: 'Consider the lilies of the field, how they grow. They don't toil, neither do they spin.'
9 Keynes (1923: 80).
10 Russell (1935).
11 Russell (1935: 13) wrote: 'I want to say, in all seriousness, that a great deal of harm is being done in the modern world by the belief in the virtuousness of work, and that the road to happiness and prosperity lies in an organised diminution of work.' It is difficult to find a clearer repudiation of the work ethic than this.
12 The false dawn for the thirty-hour working week in 1930s America is discussed in Hunnicutt (1988).
13 Skidelsky (2019) offers an overview of trends in work time during the post-war period.
14 Bregman (2018: 36–7) discusses how fear was associated with the prospect of the rise of leisure hours in the 1950s and 1960s. This fear even persisted into the 1970s and shaped a view that the coming 'leisure revolution' was not only real, but also a potential existential threat to humanity. As I show in chapter 6, fear – and hope – for the future of work have re-emerged in modern debate, thanks to a new focus on the scope for the acceleration of digital technologies.
15 Huberman and Minns (2007) discuss historical trends in work hours.
16 Schor (1992: 44) compares work hours in pre-capitalist and capitalist times.
17 All data are from the OECD website, accessed 28 June 2021: https://www.oecd-ilibrary.org/employment/data/hours

-worked/average-annual-hours-actually-worked_data-0030
3-en.

18 See the data in Skidelsky (2019: 9).

19 See the introduction to Pencavel (2018). On the 'busyness' of
the rich, see Hamermesh (2018).

20 Some argue that commute time should count as part of
normal work hours, given that it is often used to carry out
work tasks. See S. Coughlan, 'Emails While Commuting
"Should Count as Work"', *BBC*, 30 August 2018 (available
at: https://www.bbc.co.uk/news/education-45333270).

21 A. Hess, 'On Holiday: Countries with the Most Vacation
Days', *USA Today*, 8 June 2013 (available at: https://
eu.usatoday.com/story/money/business/2013/06/08/coun
tries-most-vacation-days/2400193).

22 A. Hess, 'Here's How Many Paid Vacation Days the Typical
American Worker Gets', *CNCB*, 6 July 2018 (available at:
https://www.cnbc.com/2018/07/05/heres-how-many-paid-
vacation-days-the-typical-american-worker-gets-.html).

23 S. Fernandes and R. Greene, 'Portugal Cancels Holidays after
Vatican Talks', *CNN*, 9 May 2012 (available at: https://edi
tion.cnn.com/2012/05/09/world/europe/portugal-holidays/
index.html).

24 Bregman (2018: 39).

25 Hermann (2015: 185).

26 In the UK, evidence suggests that women perform 60 per
cent more unpaid work than men. See 'Women Shoulder
the Responsibility of "Unpaid Work"', *Office for National
Statistics*, 10 November 2016 (available at: https://www.
ons.gov.uk/employmentandlabourmarket/peopleinwork/ear
ningsandworkinghours/articles/womenshouldertheresponsib
ilityofunpaidwork/2016-11-10).

27 Schulte (2014) discusses the added burdens of work –
especially those faced by women – in the modern labour
market.

28 On underemployment, see Bell and Blanchflower (2021).

29 On unmatched preferences for shorter work hours, see
Stewart and Swaffield (1997) and Reynolds and Aletraris
(2006).

30 Falls in work hours have tended to cluster in particular
periods. In the UK, Bienefeld (1972) identifies four periods
(1872–4, 1919–20, 1946–9 and 1960–6) when work hours

fell sharply. Two of these coincided with the 'golden age' of capitalism – periods in which trade union power was strong and robust economic growth enabled capitalist employers to meet workers' demands for shorter work hours. See also Skidelsky (2019).

31 Piketty (2014) and Tridico (2018) discuss the trend towards rising inequality in capitalist economies since the 1970s.

32 Glyn (2006) discusses the regressive turn in contemporary capitalist economies.

33 Friedman (2017) highlights the rise in inequality in capitalist economies as a reason why work hours have not fallen in line with Keynes's prediction.

34 Becker (1965) offers a foundation for the orthodox economic theory of time allocation.

35 Hermann (2015) shows how shifts in power (away from labour and towards capital) account for the slowdown in work time reduction over recent decades. While there remain differences in work time between countries, this slowdown represents a general trend across capitalist economies.

36 Long working weeks (in excess of forty-eight hours) and disturbed sleep patterns due to overwork were reported by those who worked from home during the COVID-19 pandemic. The concern about the lengthening in work hours has led to calls for new restrictions on work time, including a legal 'right to disconnect'. See 'Lockdown Shows Urgent Need for Workers to Have a Right to Disconnect', *European Trade Union Confederation*, 2 June 2020 (available at: https://www.etuc.org/en/pressrelease/lockdown-shows-urgent-need-workers-have-right-disconnect). The right to disconnect is also discussed in chapter 7.

37 Keynes (1963: 365).

38 There is ample evidence that many workers' preferred or desired work hours are exceeded by their actual work hours. This suggests that overwork is involuntary and is welfare-reducing. See, for example, Stewart and Swaffield (1997) and Reynolds and Aletraris (2006).

39 Freeman (2008) criticizes Keynes's 1930 essay, pointing out how Keynes failed to anticipate how performance-related pay schemes would lead workers to keep working long hours. Further, Freeman notes how, in contrast to Keynes's expectations, work has remained attractive in society,

preventing the reduction of work hours. Freeman highlights the benefits of continued working and questions Keynes's broader vision of a leisured future. I think he underestimates the direct and opportunity costs of working and the value of a life with less work. I address the costs of work more directly in chapter 4.

40 Skidelsky and Skidelsky (2012: 33–42) discuss in detail the different determinants of insatiability and their impacts on work hours.

41 Hirsch (1977) discusses the role and impacts of 'positional goods'.

42 Veblen (1994).

43 On the direct link between inequality and work hours, see Bell and Freeman (2001) and Bowles and Park (2005).

44 Cowling (2006) makes the link between higher advertising expenditure and longer work hours in modern capitalist economies.

45 Weeks (2011), Frayne (2015) and Srnicek and Williams (2015).

46 As discussed in chapter 2, the attempt to criticize and 'refuse' work seems to derive from a concern not to eulogize it, but the effect of this approach is to overlook the scope to change and transform work.

47 For a macroeconomic case for work time reduction, see LaJeunesse (2009). Short-time work schemes have also worked well during recent crises, allowing some countries (e.g. Germany) to avoid higher unemployment. The challenge is to ensure that shorter work hours are maintained in more 'normal' times and that they become an enduring basis for evening out the allocation of work in society.

48 Weeks (2011) offers a feminist argument for a shorter working week, focusing on how shorter work hours can create time for the re-evaluation and reimagination of existing gender roles.

49 For a systematic review of the evidence on the negative effects of long work hours on health, see Bannai and Tamakoshi (2014).

50 Virtanen et al. (2009).

51 Kanai (2009) discusses the phenomenon of 'karoshi'.

52 Knight et al. (2013).

53 Devetter and Rousseau (2011) discuss how work time

reduction could help to foster more sustainable forms of consumption.

54 For example, a move to a four-day work week in a New Zealand insurance company led to both higher productivity and increased employee well-being. This success has inspired calls for further trials of a four-day work week. See E. Ainge Roy, 'Work Less, Get More: New Zealand Firm's Four-Day Week an "Unmitigated Success"', *Guardian*, 19 July 2018 (available at: https://www.theguardian.com/world/2018/jul/19/work-less-get-more-new-zealand-firms-four-day-week-an-unmitigated-success).

4 Realities of Work

1 For US data on the extent of low-paid work, see M. Ross and N. Bateman, 'Meet the Low-Wage Workforce', *Brookings Institution Metropolitan Policy Program*, 7 November 2019 (available at: https://www.brookings.edu/research/meet-the-low-wage-workforce). For discussion of low pay in the UK, see Lee et al. (2018).

2 Critiques of modern work – its quality and meaning – include Fleming (2015) and Graeber (2018); the latter provides a critical focus for the discussion that follows.

3 In the UK, for example, the Taylor Review (Taylor, 2017) supported the goal of 'good work for all'. Other authors have called 'meaningful work' a 'fundamental human need' (Yeoman, 2014).

4 The thesis is set out in Graeber (2018).

5 Terkel (1974: xxix).

6 The original blog post (available at: https://www.strike.coop/bullshit-jobs) caused a stir on social media and in activist circles. In one innovative response, posters were displayed on the London Underground that featured quotes from the blog. The intention was to provoke commuters into thinking about – and ideally acting against – the meaninglessness of their jobs (Graeber, 2018: xxi).

7 The results of the survey can be found here: https://yougov.co.uk/topics/lifestyle/articles-reports/2015/08/12/british-jobs-meaningless.

8 See discussion in Graeber (2018: 63–4).

9 Graeber (2018: xvi).

10 Graeber (2018: 121–2) likens the meaninglessness of bullshit jobs to a form of torture and even sadomasochism. Those in bullshit jobs, however, face having to put up with the pain of work due to their material dependency on it. In this case, the torture is ongoing, without any safe exit.

11 Cascio et al. (2021) address the drivers and effects of downsizing in modern organizations.

12 Blanchflower (2019) explores the extent of unemployment and underemployment in contemporary capitalism.

13 Van der Zwan (2014) discusses the different dimensions of the financialization of the economy and society over recent decades.

14 Green (2006) and Green et al. (2021).

15 The survey results can be found here: https://yougov. co.uk/topics/lifestyle/articles-reports/2015/08/12/british-jobs-meaningless.

16 For discussion on the different meanings attached to work by workers, see Findlay and Thompson (2017).

17 For an overlapping critique of the bullshit jobs thesis, see Thompson and Pitts (2018).

18 Bryson and MacKerron (2017).

19 On the negative effects of unemployment on reported happiness, see Clark and Oswald (1994). See also the discussion that follows.

20 Bryson and MacKerron (2017: 109).

21 'Love-making and intimacy', by contrast, rank as the most pleasurable experience. See the full results in Bryson and MacKerron (2017: 117). Similar results are found in Kahneman et al. (2004) in a US study using a 'day reconstruction method'.

22 Bryson and MacKerron (2017: 124).

23 Formally, there is the influence of work itself on happiness (where work can be seen as a direct source of disutility) and that of work hours on happiness (where work can be regarded as a disutility because it prevents the opportunity for utility-yielding leisure hours). Spencer (2014) discusses the different conceptions of the disutility of work in economics.

24 Pfeffer's criticisms of modern work, and the organizations in which it takes place, are detailed in *Dying for a Paycheck* (Pfeffer, 2018).

25 Goh et al. (2015).
26 Bosma et al. (1997).
27 These theories include agency theory; see chapter 2.
28 Pfeffer co-authored a paper that links the teaching of economic theories in business schools with the rise of regressive forms of management in real-world organizations (Ferraro et al., 2005).
29 Spencer (2020) further criticizes the performativity thesis as applied to the teaching of 'bad' and 'good' theories of management.
30 Osterman (2019) argues that Pfeffer's 2018 book fails to show how managers may profit from 'bad' management and how the incentive for them to switch to 'good' management may remain weak. Job insecurity and low-control jobs, for example, may fit with managers' profit-maximizing strategies. Osterman, too, highlights Pfeffer's failure to discuss the need for regulation and 'countervailing power' (for example, via trade unions) to shift management practice. Ultimately, Pfeffer's focus on persuading managers to behave differently misses how broader reforms are needed to overcome the costs and pathologies of work in modern society.
31 For a discussion on the negative effects of unemployment on well-being, see Wood and Burchell (2018).
32 Jahoda (1982).
33 Clark and Oswald (1994).
34 Case and Deaton (2020).
35 Case and Deaton (2020: 8) link the destruction of work to the demise of 'working class life'.
36 Layard (2004). Layard's policy ideas influenced the UK welfare reforms implemented under New Labour (1997–2010) – reforms that made receipt of benefits conditional on constant job search. The welfare system in the UK, in general, has remained work-focused, seeking to impose sanctions on those who are deemed not to be work-ready or prepared.
37 Chandola and Zhang (2018).
38 Clark (2015) defends a subjective approach to job quality – one based on the use and application of job satisfaction data.
39 Brown et al. (2007) discuss the limitations posed by the use of subjective data (particularly job satisfaction data) for understanding the quality of work. See also Spencer (2015).

40 Felstead et al. (2019) use different data in developing an objective or needs-based approach to measuring the quality of work.

5 Demanding Better Work for All

1 This chapter builds on discussion of unequal access to high-quality work and its links to social injustice in the field of political philosophy (see e.g. Murphy, 1993; Sayer, 2009; Arnold, 2011).
2 The ideas and arguments in this chapter draw on Spencer (2013b).
3 For a discussion on the conception and measurement of 'Decent Work', see Burchell et al. (2014).
4 See the Taylor Review (Taylor, 2017). This sought to downplay the need for radical reform, arguing for a policy approach that builds 'on the distinctive strengths of our existing labour market and framework of regulation: the British way' (Taylor, 2017: 7). There is no sense here of how the deregulated model adopted in the UK may be a barrier to progressive reform in the labour market and the workplace.
5 Any standard economics textbook includes discussion of the labour supply choices made by individual workers. See, for example, Borjas (2002: ch. 6).
6 Human capital theory was originally formalized and applied in economics by Gary Becker (1964).
7 Nozick (1974: 246–50).
8 For discussion of 'adaptive preferences' in relation to the quality of work, see Elster (1986: 123).
9 Marglin (1974).
10 Braverman (1974). I take up these points in chapter 6 when I consider the political influences on the adoption and implementation of technology in the workplace.
11 Kohn and Schooler (1982).
12 Lane (1991: 240–2).
13 Bosma et al. (1997). Note here the links to Pfeffer (2018), discussed in chapter 4.
14 Schneider and Harknett (2019: 82).
15 Shapiro and Stiglitz (1984).

16 Williamson (1985).
17 Pfeffer (2007) suggests that 'win-win' outcomes can be achieved under forms of high-commitment management. These place emphasis more on autonomy than on direct control and appeal to notions of cooperation and gain-sharing. Such management may be able to sustain higher profits, but there are severe limits to progress in the quality of work, from the profit imperative. The tendency remains for firms to reduce costs and adopt coercive tactics when economic conditions turn bad or financial stakeholders exert pressure for higher economic gains. In this sense – reiterating the point made in chapter 4 – decisive progress in improving the quality of work will depend on broader structural change.
18 I address the contradictions and potentialities of techno-logical progress as a mechanism for lightening work in chapter 6.
19 Muirhead (2004: 173) discusses this option.
20 Sayer (2009: 10) gives the example of his own university establishing a new policy requiring lecturers to empty the waste bins in their offices. Placing this requirement on indi-vidual lecturers meant that they had to take responsibility for clearing up the waste they generated. Creating this con-nection between the task of emptying their bins and their everyday work helped to make the bin-emptying less oner-ous. The example illustrates how, at a broader level, tasks of different quality can be combined and how there is no necessary reason to restrict some people (e.g. cleaners) to low-quality work.
21 Sayer (2009: 11–12).
22 Gomberg (2007). See also Sayer (2009).

6 Automation and a World without Work

1 Brynjolfsson and MacAfee (2014), Ford (2015), Schwab (2016), Frey (2019) and Susskind (2020).
2 The empirical study by Frey and Osborne (2017) has become the single most-cited reference on the prospects for the loss of work through automation. Its prediction of a near halv-ing in US employment over the next twenty years has been

widely reported. Originally published as a working paper, this study has since become a peer-reviewed article, shaping debate in both academia and policy circles.

3 Most authors take a positive view on the long-run effects of technology, but argue that it will cause disruption in the short and medium terms that will require reforms within society (e.g. Brynjolfsson and McAfee 2014; Susskind 2020). A more pessimistic view – one predicting negative consequences of automation and the potential for long-lasting economic and social damage from 'the rise of the robots' – can be found in Ford (2015).

4 Mason (2015) and Srnicek and Williams (2015).

5 Mokyr et al. (2015) offer a historical overview of debates on automation, including the persistent worry that technology will destroy jobs.

6 Mill's own view, as noted in chapter 2, was that society needed to relinquish the quest for ever higher economic growth and instead focus on using productivity gains to extend leisure time. He also believed in the need for greater worker ownership and even contemplated the merits of socialism as an alternative to capitalism (see Spencer 2009: 26–30). These views, again, brought him into conflict with other classical economists, though they allowed him to connect with social reformers who argued that capitalism was failing to meet the needs of the working class.

7 Bregman (2018: 36–7).

8 Rifkin (1995). For an overview of debates on automation and the future of work and leisure, see Granter (2008).

9 Susskind and Susskind (2015) discuss the effects of digital technologies on work and employment in the legal profession.

10 Turner (2018) and Susskind (2020), for example, highlight what they see as the inexorable progress of digital technologies and predict that this will severely limit employment in the future.

11 Haldane (2015).

12 Frey and Osborne (2015).

13 Arntz et al. (2017), for example, estimate that 9 per cent of US jobs could be automated (a much lower estimate than Frey and Osborne's 47 per cent).

14 Brynjolfsson and McAfee (2014).

15 Srnicek and Williams (2015). For a similar radical perspective on automation, see Mason (2015).

16 Fleming (2019) highlights the ubiquity of work in modern society. He also refers to barriers to automation.

17 The UK is a good example. An underlying problem in the UK is one of 'too few robots', with low investment in technology underpinning a low-productivity and low-wage economy (Spencer and Slater, 2020).

18 Huws (2014) discusses the job-creating potential of new digital technologies.

19 The discussion here draws on Spencer (2018).

20 Bergvall-Kåreborn and Howcroft (2014).

21 Woodcock and Graham (2020) discuss the nature, evolution and effects of the gig economy.

22 Employees in companies such as Uber have had to launch legal cases to secure their basic rights and even after winning court cases have faced hostility from employers to extend their rights at work. Missing has been any wider legislation to regulate the gig economy. See P. Inman, 'After Uber's U-turn, Ministers Must Stop Giving Gig Economy Bosses an Easy Ride', *Guardian*, 21 March 2021 (available at: https://www.theguardian.com/business/2021/mar/21/aft er-uber-u-turn-ministers-must-stop-giving-gig-economy-bos ses-an-easy-ride).

23 Schumpeter, 'Digital Taylorism', *The Economist*, 12 September 2005 (available at: http://www.economist.com/ news/business/21664190-modern-version-scientific-manage ment-threatens-dehumanise-workplace-digital).

24 W. Evans, 'How Amazon Hid its Safety Crisis', *Centre for Investigative Reporting*, 22 September 2020 (available at: https://revealnews.org/article/how-amazon-hid-its-safety-crisis).

25 C. Drury, 'Amazon Workers "Forced to Urinate in Plastic Bottles Because They Cannot Go to Toilet on Shift"', *Independent*, 19 July 2019 (available at: https://www.independent.co.uk/news/uk/home-news/ amazon-protests-workers-urinate-plastic-bottles-no-toilet-breaks-milton-keynes-jeff-bezos-a9012351.html).

26 S. O'Connor, 'Why I Was Wrong to Be Optimistic about Robots', *Financial Times*, 9 February 2021 (available at: https://www. ft.com/content/087fce16-3924-4348-8390-235b435c53b2).

27 Brynjolfsson and McAfee (2014: 234).
28 Brynjolfsson and McAfee (2014: 182).
29 See the discussion in chapter 3 as well as Coote et al. (2020) on the merits of work time reduction. These are re-emphasized in chapter 7, in support of the move to a four-day work week.
30 Brynjolfsson and McAfee (2014: 234).
31 Srnicek and Williams (2015: 126). Using florid language, some authors call for a 'fully automated luxury communism' (Bastani, 2019).
32 Thompson (2020) offers further criticisms of post-work politics.
33 See Weeks (2011: 12, 109).
34 R. Freeman, 'Who Owns the Robots Rules the World', *IZA World of Labor*, 2015 (available at: https://wol.iza.org/arti cles/who-owns-the-robots-rules-the-world/long).

7 *Working for Change*

1 The abstractness of the concept of GDP is reflected in the fact that not many people (outside economics) understand what it means. Here GDP has rhetorical force as a symbol and measure of the economy, but lacks clear meaning in the wider public realm. See C. Giles, 'Britons Understand Little About Economics, Report Finds', *Financial Times*, 25 November 2020 (available at: https://www.ft.com/con tent/93821297-96ea-4286-8f01-ccb6fa09161f).
2 Simon Kuznets, who famously pioneered national income accounting, was well aware of the limits to GDP as a measure of progress. Famously, he wrote that 'the welfare of a nation can scarcely be inferred from a measure of national income' (Kuznets, 1934: 7). Yet generations of economists have proceeded as if GDP is the main or only measure of welfare. The concept has been elevated to the centre of attention, despite its limitations.
3 See, for example, Messac (2018).
4 A key writer here is the economist Richard Layard, who has published several books on the meaning and importance of happiness. See, for example, Layard (2005) and Layard and Ward (2020).

5 See Stiglitz et al. (2018).

6 Alternative theories move the focus away from subjective well-being and instead emphasize the objective conditions faced by people in their lives – they allow for consideration of adaptation to adversity and the potential and actual unreliability of measures of reported happiness as indicators of well-being. One example is the capabilities framework of Amartya Sen and Martha Nussbaum (Sen, 1999; Sen and Nussbaum, 1993).

7 See, for example, the work of Stevenson and Wolfers (2008), which finds a positive relationship between economic growth and subjective well-being. Here the debate is less about the objectives of the economy than on the robustness of empirical evidence linking economic growth and reported happiness. In this case, the scope for change in policy and the economy is narrowed significantly.

8 Glyn (2006) discusses the crisis-prone nature of capitalist economies since the 1970s. For a discussion of the global financial crisis of 2007–8 and its aftermath, see Tooze (2018).

9 See also the discussion in chapter 3, 'Power matters'.

10 Montgomerie (2019).

11 There is a somewhat similar reading of Keynes – one that links Keynes to the idea of a post-scarcity and workless utopia – in Skidelsky and Skidelsky (2012).

12 Kalecki (1943: 331).

13 Keynes (1936: 129). Keynes favoured investment by the state in activities with high social value, including house-building.

14 R. Partington, 'More Than a Third of UK Workers "Risk Health in Low-Quality Jobs"', *Guardian*, 4 February 2020 (available at: https://www.theguardian.com/money/2020/feb/04/more-than-a-third-of-uk-workers-risk-health-in-low-quality-jobs).

15 D. Susskind, 'Universal Basic Income Is an Affordable and Feasible Response to Coronavirus', *Financial Times*, 18 March 2020 (available at: https://www.ft.com/content/927d28e0-6847-11eaa6ac-9122541af204).

16 Friedman (1962).

17 C. Weller, 'Elon Musk Doubles Down on Universal Basic Income: "It's Going to be Necessary"', *Business Insider*, 13 February 2017 (available at: https://www.businessin

sider.com/elon-musk-universal-basic-income-2017-2?r=US
&IR=T).

18 For a critical (post-work) argument for a UBI, see Weeks
    (2011), Srnicek and Williams (2015) and Graeber (2018).

19 In countries where a UBI has been trialled, the amount of
    money received by individuals has been relatively modest.
    Indeed, trials have been set up in ways that do not disturb
    the need and incentive for workers to take paid work. A pilot
    scheme in Finland, for example, aimed at getting people into
    work, undermining any wider goal of extending freedom
    from work. The point is that any significant UBI would
    probably be resisted by employers. A UBI with emancipation
    at its core would require wider structural reform – beyond a
    level that most employers would want to see implemented.
    In the meantime, there is the danger that a UBI will be
    used to retrench the welfare state and to subsidize more
    paid work, denying any radical vision of the future. For an
    account of the Finnish UBI trial, see A. Nagesh, 'Finland
    Basic Income Trial Left People "Happier But Jobless"', *BBC*,
    8 February 2019 (available at: https://www.bbc.co.uk/news/
    world-europe-47169549).

20 These points are raised by Muirhead (2004: 19).

21 See the contribution by Standing (2017), for example.

22 For arguments in support of a four-day work week, see
    Skidelsky (2019) and Coote et al. (2020). I propose here
    a four-day work week as an initial goal and do not rule
    out further reductions in work time beyond this level. The
    point is to secure the shortest number of work hours that is
    conducive to the highest level of well-being.

23 Skidelsky (2019) proposes a sector-by-sector approach to
    work time reduction, supported by a 'job guarantee pro-
    gramme' (to facilitate the move to full employment) and new
    forms of social partnership (to help extend shorter working
    hours from the public sector to the private sector).

24 A legal 'right to disconnect' has been implemented in
    some EU countries and has gained popularity as a policy
    idea in the context of the COVID-19 crisis, as work and
    home life have merged. See P. Yeung, '"If You Switch Off,
    People Think You're Lazy": Demands Grow for a Right
    to Disconnect from Work', *Guardian*, 10 February 2021
    (available at: https://www.theguardian.com/world/2021/feb/

10/if-you-switch-off-people-think-youre-lazy-demands-grow-for-a-right-to-disconnect-from-work).

25 See discussion in Skidelsky (2019: 44–7).

26 Coote et al. (2020: 112) make this recommendation, suggesting that the mandate of a new Working Time Commission 'would be to map out a consensual path towards increased statutory paid time off in return for slower future pay growth overall'.

27 In the UK, the Trades Union Congress (TUC) has renewed the call for shorter work hours (indeed, it has backed the demand for a four-day work week) and one union – the Communication Workers Union – has secured a cut in the working week for its members. See K. Allen, 'A Four-Day Week with Decent Pay for All? It's the Future', *TUC*, 30 July 2019 (available at: https://www.tuc.org.uk/blogs/four-day-week-decent-pay-all-its-future).

28 Skidelsky and Skidelsky (2012: 208–11).

29 In 2020, a group of academics called for the democratization of work. See N. Fraser, S. Neiman, C. Mouffe, S. Sassen, J-W. Müller, D. Rodrik, T. Piketty, G. Zucman, H-J. Chang and many others, 'Humans Are Not Resources: Coronavirus Shows Why We Must Democratise Work', *Guardian*, 15 May 2020 (available at: https://www.theguardian.com/commentisfree/2020/may/15/humans-resources-coronavirus-democratise-work-health-lives-market).

30 On the case for greater democracy in workplaces and the wider economy, see Cumbers (2020).

31 For an example of a Green New Deal in the UK context, see 'Labour's Green Transformation Fund', *Labour Party*, 2019 (available at: https://labour.org.uk/wp-content/uploads/2019/11/Green-Transformation-Fund.pdf).

32 Ideas of reimagining the economy on the basis of sustainability goals have featured in the modern 'degrowth' literature. See, for example, Hickel (2020).

33 See Mazzucato (2021).

34 Skidelsky (2019).

35 Tcherneva (2020) offers an extended argument for a job guarantee scheme, showing how it might operate on a voluntary and universal basis and on terms that facilitate social and economic development, particularly at the local level.

36 Morris (1993b: 296).

8 Conclusion

1 For a discussion of the negative consequences of homeworking, see J. Harris, 'Homeworking Sounds Good – Until Your Job Takes Over Your Life', *Guardian*, 7 March 2021 (available at: https://www.theguardian.com/commentisfree/2021/mar/07/homeworking-job-takes-over-life-office-grind-remote-working).
2 B. Staton, 'The Upstart Unions Taking on the Gig Economy and Outsourcing', *Financial Times*, 19 January 2020 (available at: https://www.ft.com/content/576c68ea-3784-11ea-a6d3-9a26f8c3cba4?shareType=nongift).
3 In the UK, for example, the TUC has pledged support for a four-day work week (TUC, 2018). A similar pledge was included in the manifesto of the UK Labour Party for the December 2019 general election.
4 There now exists a 'four-day work week campaign' (https://www.4dayweek.co.uk).
5 The government in Spain announced in March 2021 that it would trial a four-day week – this came after successful lobbying from one political party. See A. Kassam, 'Spain to Launch Trial of Four-Day Working Week', 15 March 2021 (available at: https://www.theguardian.com/world/2021/mar/15/spain-to-launch-trial-of-four-day-working-week).

References

Anthony, P. (1977) *The Ideology of Work*, London: Tavistock.

Arnold, S. (2011) 'The Difference Principle at Work', *Journal of Political Philosophy*, 20(1): 94–118.

Arntz, M., Gregory, T. and Zierahn, U. (2017) 'Revisiting the Risk of Automation', *Economics Letters*, 159: 157–60.

Bannai, A. and Tamakoshi, A. (2014) 'The Association Between Long Working Hours and Health: A Systematic Review of Epidemiological Evidence', *Scandinavian Journal of Work, Environment and Health*, 40(1): 5–18.

Bastani, A. (2019) *Fully Automated Luxury Communism: A Manifesto*, London: Verso.

Becker, G. (1964) *Human Capital*, New York: Columbia University Press.

Becker, G. (1965) 'A Theory of the Allocation of Time', *Economic Journal*, 75(299): 493–517.

Bell, D. and Blanchflower, D. (2021) 'Underemployment in the United States and Europe', *Industrial and Labor Relations Review*, 74(1): 56–94.

Bell, L. and Freeman, R. (2001) 'The Incentive for Working Hard: Explaining Hours Worked Differences in the US and Germany', *Labour Economics*, 8(2): 181–202.

Bellamy, E. (1951) *Looking Backward: 2000–1887*, New York: Modern Library.

Bellamy Foster, J. (2017) 'The Meaning of Work in a Sustainable Society', *Monthly Review*, 69(4): 1–14.

Bentham, J. (1983) *The Collected Works of Jeremy Bentham: Deontology together with A Table of the Springs of Action and Article on Utilitarianism*, A. Goldworth (ed.), Oxford: Clarendon Press.

Bergvall-Kåreborn, B. and Howcroft, D. (2014) 'Amazon Mechanical Turk and the Commodification of Labour', *New Technology, Work and Employment*, 29(3): 213–23.

Bienefeld, M. (1972) *Working Hours in British Industry: An Economic History*, London School of Economics Research Monograph, Trowbridge: Redwood Press.

Blanchflower, D. (2019) *Not Working: Where Have All the Good Jobs Gone?*, Princeton: Princeton University Press.

Borjas, G. (2002) *Labor Economics* (2nd edn), New York: McGraw-Hill.

Bosma, H., Marmot, M., Hemingway, H., Nicholson, A., Brunner, E. and Stanfeld, S. (1997) 'Low Job Control and Risk of Coronary Heart Disease in the Whitehall II (Prospective Cohort) Study', *British Medical Journal*, 314: 558–65.

Bowles, S. and Park, Y. (2005) 'Emulation, Inequality, and Work Hours: Was Thorstein Veblen Right?', *Economic Journal*, 115(507): 397–412.

Braverman, H. (1974) *Labor and Monopoly Capital*, New York: Monthly Review Press.

Bregman, R. (2018) *Utopia for Realists: And How We Can Get There*, London: Bloomsbury.

Brown, A., Charlwood, A., Forde, C. and Spencer, D. (2007) 'Job Quality and the Economics of New Labour: A Critical Appraisal Using Subjective Survey Data', *Cambridge Journal of Economics*, 31(6): 941–71.

Brynjolfsson, E. and McAfee, A. (2014) *The Second Machine Age: Work, Progress, and Prosperity in a Time of Brilliant Technologies*, New York: Norton.

Bryson, A. and MacKerron G. (2017) 'Are You Happy While You Work?', *Economic Journal*, 127(599): 106–25.

Budd, J. (2011) *The Thought of Work*, Ithaca: Cornell University Press.

Burawoy, M. (1979) *Manufacturing Consent: Changes in the Labor Process Under Monopoly Capitalism*, Chicago: University of Chicago Press.

Burchell, B., Sehnbruch, K., Piasna, A. and Agloni, N. (2014) 'The Quality of Employment and Decent Work: Definitions, Methodologies, and Ongoing Debates', *Cambridge Journal of Economics*, 38(2): 459–77.

Carlyle, T. (1843) *Past and Present*, London: Chapman and Hall.

Carlyle, T. (1849) 'The Nigger Question', reprinted in *Thomas Carlyle: Critical and Miscellaneous Essays* (1899), vol. 4, London: Chapman and Hall, 348–83.

Cascio, W., Chatrath, A. and Christie-David, R. (2021) 'Antecedents and Consequences of Employment and Asset Restructuring', *Academy of Management Journal*, 64(2): 587–613.

Case, A. and Deaton, A. (2020) *Deaths of Despair and the Future of Capitalism*, Princeton: Princeton University Press.

Chandola, T. and Zhang, N. (2018) 'Re-Employment, Job Quality, Health and Allostatic Load Biomarkers: Prospective Evidence from the UK Household Longitudinal Study', *International Journal of Epidemiology*, 47(1): 47–57.

Clark, A. (2015) 'What Makes a Good Job? Job Quality and Job Satisfaction', *IZA World of Labor* (available at: https://wol.iza.org/uploads/articles/215/pdfs/what-makes-good-job-job-quality-and-job-satisfaction.pdf).

Clark, A. and Oswald, A. (1994) 'Unhappiness and Unemployment', *Economic Journal*, 104(2): 648–59.

Coats, A. (1958) 'Changing Attitudes to Labour in the Mid-Eighteenth Century', *Economic History Review*, 11(1): 35–51.

Coats, A. (1967) 'The Classical Economists and the Labourer', in E. L. Jones and G. E. Mingay (eds.), *Land, Labour and Population in the Industrial Revolution*, London: Edward Arnold, 100–30.

Cohen, J. (2018) *Not Working: Why We Have to Stop*, London: Granta.

Coote, A., Harper, A., and Stirling, A. (2020) *The Case for a Four-Day Week*, London: Polity.

Cowling, K. (2006) 'Prosperity, Depression and Modern Capitalism', *Kyklos*, 59(3): 369–81.

Cumbers, A. (2020) *The Case for Economic Democracy*, London: Polity.

Defoe, D. (1704) *Giving Alms No Charity and Employing the Poor a Grievance to the Nation*, London: n.p.

Devetter, F-X. and Rousseau, S. (2011) 'Working Hours and Sustainable Development', *Review of Social Economy*, 69(3): 333–55.

Elster, J. (1986) 'Self-Realization in Work and Politics: The Marxist Conception of the Good Life', *Social Philosophy and Policy*, 3(2): 97–126.

Felstead, A., Gallie, D., Green, F. and Henseke, G. (2019) 'Conceiving, Designing and Trailing a Short-Form Measure of Job Quality: A Proof-of-Concept Study', *Industrial Relations Journal*, 50(1): 2–19.

Ferraro, F., Pfeffer, J. and Sutton, R. (2005) 'Economics Language and Assumptions: How Theories can Become Self-Fulfilling', *Academy of Management Review*, 30(1): 8–24.

Findlay, P. and Thompson, P. (2017) 'Contemporary Work: Its Meanings and Demands', *Journal of Industrial Relations*, 59(2): 122–38.

Fleming, P. (2015) *The Mythology of Work: How Capitalism Persists Despite Itself*, London: Pluto.

Fleming, P. (2019) 'Robots and Organization Studies: Why Robots Might Not Want to Steal Your Job', *Organization Studies*, 40(1): 23–38.

Ford, M. (2015) *The Rise of the Robots: Technology and the Threat of Mass Unemployment*, London: Oneworld.

Frayne, D. (2015) *The Refusal of Work: The Theory and Practice of Resistance to Work*, London: Zed Books.

Freeman, R. (2008) 'Why Do We Work More than Keynes Expected?', in L. Pecchi and G. Piga (eds.), *Revisiting Keynes: Economic Possibilities for Our Grandchildren*, Cambridge, MA: MIT Press, 135–42.

Frey, C. (2019) *The Technology Trap: Capital, Labor, and Power in the Age of Automation*, Princeton: Princeton University Press.

Frey, C. and Osborne, M. (2015) *Technology at Work*, Oxford: Citi GPS.

Frey, C. and Osborne, M. (2017) 'The Future of Employment: How Susceptible Are Jobs to Computerisation?', *Technological Forecasting and Social Change*, 114: 254–80.

Friedman, B. (2017) 'Work and Consumption in an Era of Unbalanced Technological Advance', *Journal of Evolutionary Economics*, 27(2): 221–37.

Friedman, M. (1962) *Capitalism and Freedom*, Chicago: Chicago University of Press.

Furniss, E. (1920) *The Position of the Labourer in a System of Nationalism*, New York: Houghton Mifflin.

Glyn, A. (2006) *Capitalism Unleashed*, Oxford: Oxford University Press.

Goh, J., Pfeffer, J. and Zenios, S. (2015) 'The Relationship Between Workplace Stressors and Mortality and Health Costs in the United States', *Management Science*, 62(2): 608–28.

Gomberg, P. (2007) *How to Make Opportunity Equal*, New York: Blackwell.

Gorz, A. (1985) *Paths to Paradise: On the Liberation from Work*, London: Pluto Press.

Graeber, D. (2018) *Bullshit Jobs: A Theory*, London: Allen Lane.

Granter, E. (2008) 'A Dream of Ease: Situating the Future of Work and Leisure', *Futures*, 40(9): 803–11.

Granter, E. (2009) *Critical Social Theory and the End of Work*, Farnham: Ashgate.

Green, F. (2006) *Demanding Work: The Paradox of Job Quality in the Affluent Society*, Princeton: Princeton University Press.

Green, F., Felstead, A., Gallie, D. and Henseke, G. (2021) 'Working Still Harder', *Industrial and Labor Relations Review*, forthcoming.

Haldane, A. (2015) 'Labour's Share', Speech at the Trades Union Congress, London, 12 November (available at: https://www.bankofengland.co.uk/speech/2015/labours-share).

Hamermesh, D. (2018) *Spending Time: The Most Valuable Resource*, New York: Oxford University Press.

Hatcher, J. (1998) 'Labour, Leisure and Economic Thought before the Nineteenth Century', *Past and Present*, 160: 64–115.

Hermann, C. (2015) *Capitalism and the Political Economy of Work Time*, London: Routledge.

Hickel, J. (2020) *Less is More: How Degrowth Will Save the World*, London: Penguin.

Hirsch, F. (1977) *The Social Limits to Growth*, London: Routledge.

Huberman, M. and Minns, C. (2007) 'The Times They Are Not Changin'': Days and Hours of Work in Old and New Worlds, 1870–2000', *Explorations in Economic History*, 44(4): 538–67.

Hunnicutt, B. (1988) *Work Without End: Abandoning Shorter Hours for the Right to Work*, Philadelphia: Temple University Press.

Huws, U. (2014) *Labor in the Global Digital Economy*, New York: Monthly Review Press.

Jahoda, M. (1982) *Employment and Unemployment: A Social-Psychological Analysis*, Cambridge: Cambridge University Press.

Kahneman, D., Krueger, A., Schkade, D., Schwarz, N. and Stone, A. (2004) 'A Survey Method for Characterizing Daily Life Experience: The Day Reconstruction Method', *Science*, 306(5702): 1776–80.

Kalecki, M. (1943) 'Political Aspects of Full Employment', *Political Quarterly*, 14(4): 322–31.

Kanai, A. (2009) '"Karoshi (Work to Death)" in Japan', *Journal of Business Ethics*, 84(2): 209–16.

Keynes, J. M. (1923) *A Tract on Monetary Reform*, London: Macmillan.

Keynes, J. M. (1936) *The General Theory of Employment, Interest, and Money*, London: Macmillan.

Keynes, J. M. (1963) 'Economic Possibilities for Our Grandchildren', in *Essays in Persuasion*, New York; London: Norton, 358–73.

Knight, K., Rosa, E. and Schor, J. (2013) 'Could Working Less Reduce Pressures on the Environment? A Cross-National Panel Analysis of OECD Countries, 1970–2007', *Global Environmental Change*, 23(4): 691–700.

Kohn, M. and Schooler, C. (1982) 'Job Conditions and Personality: A Longitudinal Assessment of their Reciprocal Effects', *American Journal of Sociology*, 87(6): 1257–86.

Komlosy, A. (2018) *Work: The Last 100 Years*, London: Verso.

Kuznets, S. (1934) 'National Income, 1929–1932', 73rd US Congress, Second Session, Senate Document Number 124 (available at: https://www.nber.org/system/files/chapters/c2258/c2258.pdf).

LaJeunesse, R. (2009) *Work Time Regulation as a Sustainable Full Employment Strategy*, London: Routledge.

Lane, R. (1991) *The Market Experience*, Cambridge: Cambridge University Press.

Layard, R. (2004) 'Good Jobs and Bad Jobs', Centre for Economic Performance Occasional Paper, no. 19.

Layard, R. (2005) *Happiness: Lessons from a New Science*, London: Penguin.

Layard, R. and Ward, G. (2020) *Can We Be Happier? Evidence and Ethics*, London: Penguin.

Lazear, E. and Shaw, K. (2007) 'Personnel Economics: The Economist's View of Human Resources', *Journal of Economic Perspectives*, 21(4): 91–114.

Lee, N., Green, A. and Sissons, P. (2018) 'Low-Pay Sectors, Earnings Mobility and Economic Policy in the UK', *Policy and Politics*, 46(3): 347–69.

Locke, J. (1706) 'Of the Conduct of the Understanding', in *Posthumous Works of Mr. John Locke*, London: printed by W. B. for A. and J. Churchill at the Black Swan in Paternoster Row.

Malthus, T. R. (1926) *An Essay on the Principle of Population*, London: Macmillan.

Marglin, S. (1974) 'What Do Bosses Do? The Origins and Function of Hierarchy in Capitalist Production', *Review of Radical Political Economics*, 6(2): 60–112.

Marmot, M., Allen, J., Goldblatt, P., Herd, E. and Morrison J. (2020) *Build Back Fairer: The COVID-19 Marmot Review. The Pandemic, Socioeconomic and Health Inequalities in England*, London: Institute of Health Equity.

Martin, C. (2015) 'Equity, Besides: Adam Smith and the Utility of Poverty', *Journal of the History of Economic Thought*, 37(4): 559–81.

Marx, K. (1972) *Theories of Surplus Value*, part 3, London: Lawrence and Wishart.

Marx, K. (1973) *Grundrisse*, Harmondsworth: Penguin.

Marx, K. (1975) 'Comments on James Mill', in *Marx and Engels: Collected Works*, vol. 3, London: Lawrence and Wishart, 211–28.

Marx, K. (1976) *Capital*, vol. 1, London: Penguin.

Marx, K. (1977) *Economic and Philosophic Manuscripts*, London: Lawrence and Wishart.

Marx, K. (1992) *Capital*, vol. 3, London: Penguin.

Marx, K. and Engels, F. (1976) *The German Ideology*, Moscow: Progress.

Mason, P. (2015) *Postcapitalism: A Guide to Our Future*, London: Allen Lane.

Mazzucato, M. (2021) *Mission Economy: A Moonshot Guide to Changing Capitalism*, London: Allen Lane.

Messac, L. (2018) 'Outside the Economy: Women's Work and Feminist Economics in the Construction and Critique of National Income Accounting', *Journal of Imperial and Commonwealth History*, 46(3): 552–78.

Mill, J. S. (1965) *Principles of Political Economy with Some of their Applications to Social Philosophy*, in J. Robson (ed.), *Collected Works of John Stuart Mill*, vols. 2 and 3, Toronto: University of Toronto Press.

Mill, J. S. (1984) 'The Negro Question', in J. Robson (ed.), *Collected Works of John Stuart Mill*, vol. 11, Toronto: University of Toronto Press, 85–95.

Mokyr, J., Vickers, C. and Ziebarth, N. (2015) 'The History of Technological Anxiety and the Future of Economic Growth: Is this Time Different?', *Journal of Economic Perspectives*, 29(3): 31–50.

Montgomerie, J. (2019) *Should We Abolish Household Debt?*, Cambridge: Polity.

Morris, W. (1979) 'How We Live and How We Might Live', in A. Morton (ed.), *Political Writings of William Morris*, New York: International, 134–58.

Morris, W. (1993a) 'Preface to *The Nature of Gothic* by

John Ruskin', in C. Wilmer (ed.), *News From Nowhere and Other Writings*, London: Penguin, 365–9.

Morris, W. (1993b) 'Useful Work *versus* Useless Toil', in C. Wilmer (ed.), *News From Nowhere and Other Writings*, London: Penguin, 285–306.

Morris, W. (1993c) 'The Hopes of Civilisation', in C. Wilmer (ed.), *News From Nowhere and Other Writings*, London: Penguin, 307–28.

Morris, W. (1993d) '"Looking Backward": A Review of *Looking Backward* by Edward Bellamy', in C. Wilmer (ed.), *News from Nowhere and Other Writings*, London: Penguin, 351–7.

Muirhead, R. (2004) *Just Work*, Cambridge, MA: Harvard University Press.

Murphy, J. (1993) *The Moral Economy of Labor: Aristotelian Themes in Economic Theory*, New Haven: Yale University Press.

Nozick, R. (1974) *Anarchy, State, and Utopia*, New York: Basic Books.

Osterman, P. (2019) 'Book Review: *Dying for a Paycheck: How Modern Management Harms Employee Health and Company Performance – and What We Can Do About It*', *Industrial and Labor Relations Review*, 72(5): 1278–9.

Pencavel, J. (2018) *Diminishing Returns at Work: The Consequences of Long Working Hours*, Oxford: Oxford University Press.

Perelman, M. (2010) 'Adam Smith: Class, Labor, and the Industrial Revolution', *Journal of Economic Behavior and Organization*, 76(3): 481–96.

Pfeffer, J. (2007) 'Human Resources from an Organizational Behavior Perspective: Some Paradoxes Explained', *Journal of Economic Perspectives*, 21(4): 115–34.

Pfeffer, J. (2018) *Dying for a Paycheck: How Modern Management Harms Employee Health and Company Performance – and What We Can Do About It*, New York: Harper Business.

Picchio, M., Suetens, S. and van Ours, J. (2018) 'Labour Supply Effects of Winning a Lottery', *Economic Journal*, 128(611): 1700–29.

Piketty, T. (2014) *Capital in the Twenty-First Century*, Cambridge, MA: Harvard University Press.

Reynolds, J. and Aletraris, L. (2006) 'Pursuing Preferences: The Creation and Resolution of Work Hour Mismatches', *American Sociological Review*, 71(4): 618–38.

Rifkin, J. (1995) *The End of Work: The Decline of the Global Labor Force and the Dawn of the Post-Market Era*, New York: Putnam.

Russell, B. (1935) *In Praise of Idleness*, London: Unwin Hyman.

Sayer, A. (2009) 'Contributive Justice and Meaningful Work', *Res Publica*, 15: 1–16.

Schneider, D. and Harknett, K. (2019) 'Consequences of Routine Work-Schedule Instability for Worker Health and Well-Being', *American Sociological Review*, 84(1): 82–114.

Schor, J. (1992) *The Overworked American: The Unexpected Decline of Leisure*, New York: Basic Books.

Schulte, B. (2014) *Overwhelmed: Work, Love and Play When No One Has the Time*, London: Bloomsbury.

Schwab, K. (2016) *The Fourth Industrial Revolution*, Geneva: World Economic Forum.

Sen, A. (1999) *Development as Freedom*, Oxford: Oxford University Press.

Sen, A. and Nussbaum, M. (1993) *The Quality of Life*, Oxford: Oxford University Press.

Shapiro, C. and Stiglitz, J. (1984) 'Equilibrium Unemployment as a Worker Discipline Device', *American Economic Review*, 74(3): 433–44.

Skidelsky, R. (2019) *How to Achieve Shorter Working Hours*, Progressive Economy Forum (available at: https://progressiveeconomyforum.com/wp-content/uplo ads/2019/08/PEF_Skidelsky_How_to_achieve_shorter_ working_hours.pdf).

Skidelsky, R. and Skidelsky, E. (2012) *How Much is Enough? Money and the Good Life*, London: Allen Lane.

Smith, A. (1976) *An Inquiry into the Nature and Causes of the Wealth of Nations*, R. H. Campbell and A. S. Skinner (eds.), Oxford: Clarendon Press.

Spencer, D. A. (2009) *The Political Economy of Work*, London: Routledge.

Spencer, D. A. (2013a) 'Barbarians at the Gate: A Critical Appraisal of the Influence of Economics on the Field and Practice of HRM', *Human Resource Management Journal*, 23(4): 346–59.

Spencer, D. A. (2013b) 'Promoting High Quality Work: Obstacles and Opportunities', *Journal of Business Ethics*, 114(3): 583–97.

Spencer, D. A. (2014) 'Conceptualising Work in Economics: Negating a Disutility', *Kyklos*, 67(2): 280–94.

Spencer, D. A. (2015) 'Developing an Understanding of Meaningful Work in Economics: The Case for a Heterodox Economics of Work', *Cambridge Journal of Economics*, 39(3): 675–88.

Spencer, D. A. (2018) 'Fear and Hope in an Age of Mass Automation: Debating the Future of Work', *New Technology, Work and Employment*, 33(1): 1–12.

Spencer, D. A. (2020) 'Economics and "Bad" Management: The Limits to Performativity', *Cambridge Journal of Economics*, 44(1): 17–32.

Spencer, D. and Slater, G. (2020) 'No Automation Please, We're British: Technology and the Prospects for Work', *Cambridge Journal of Regions, Economy and Society*, 13(1): 117–34.

Srnicek, N. and Williams A. (2015) *Inventing the Future: Postcapitalism and a World Without Work*, London: Verso.

Standing, G. (2017) *Basic Income: And How We Make It Happen*, London: Penguin.

Stevenson, B. and Wolfers, J. (2008) 'Economic Growth and Subjective Well-Being: Reassessing the Easterlin Paradox', *Brookings Papers on Economic Activity*, 39(1): 1–102.

Stewart, M. and Swaffield, J. (1997) 'Constraints on the Desired Hours of Work of British Men', *Economic Journal*, 107(441): 520–35.

Stiglitz, J., Fitoussi, J. and Durand, M. (2018) *Beyond GDP: Measuring What Counts for Economic and Social Performance*, Paris: OECD (available at: http://www.

oecd.org/corruption/beyond-gdp-9789264307292-en. htm).

Susskind, D. (2020) *A World Without Work: Technology, Automation and How We Should Respond*, London: Allen Lane.

Susskind, R. and Susskind, D. (2015) *The Future of the Professions: How Technology Will Transform the Work of Human Experts*, Oxford: Oxford University Press.

Taylor, M. (2017) *Good Work: The Taylor Review of Modern Working Practices*, London: Department for Business, Energy and Industrial Strategy.

Tcherneva, P. (2020) *The Case for a Job Guarantee*, London: Polity.

Terkel, S. (1974) *Working: People Talk About What They Do All Day and How They Feel About What They Do*, New York: New Press.

Thomas, K. (2009) *The Ends of Life: Roads to Fulfilment in Early Modern England*, Oxford: Oxford University Press.

Thompson, E. P. (1967) 'Time, Work-Discipline, and Industrial Capitalism', *Past and Present*, 38: 56–97.

Thompson, E. P. (1976) *William Morris: Romantic to Revolutionary*, New York: Pantheon.

Thompson, P. (2020) 'Capitalism, Technology and Work: Interrogating the Tipping Point Thesis', *Political Quarterly*, 91: 299–309.

Thompson, P. and Pitts, H. (2018) 'Bullshit About Jobs', London: Royal Society of Arts (available at: https:// www.thersa.org/blog/2018/07/bullshit-about-jobs).

Tokumitsu, M. (2015) *Do What You Love: And Other Lies About Success and Happiness*, New York: Regan Arts.

Tooze, A. (2018) *Crashed: How a Decade of Financial Crises Changed the World*, London: Penguin.

Tridico, P. (2018) 'The Determinants of Income Inequality in OECD Countries', *Cambridge Journal of Economics*, 42(4): 1009–42.

TUC (2018) *A Future that Works for Working People* (available at: https://www.tuc.org.uk/research-analysis/ reports/future-works-working-people).

Turner, A. (2018) 'Capitalism in the Age of Robots: Work,

Income and Wealth in the 21st-Century', Lecture at School of Advanced International Studies, Johns Hopkins University (available at: https://www.ineteconomics.org/research/research-papers/capitalism-in-the-age-of-robots-work-income-and-wealth-in-the-21st-century).

Van der Zwan, N. (2014) 'Making Sense of Financialization', *Socio-Economic Review*, 12(1): 99–129.

Veblen, T. (1994) *The Theory of the Leisure Class*, New York: Dover.

Virtanen, M., Singh-Manoux, A., Ferrie, J., Gimeno, D., Marmot, M., Elovainio, M., Jokela, M., Vahtera, J. and Kivimäki, M. (2009) 'Long Working Hours and Cognitive Function: The Whitehall II Study', *American Journal of Epidemiology*, 169(5): 596–605.

Vonnegut, K. (1952) *Player Piano*, New York: Laurel.

Weber, M. (1958) *The Protestant Ethic and the Spirit of Capitalism*, New York: Charles Scribner's Sons.

Weeks, K. (2011) *The Problem with Work: Feminism, Marxism, Antiwork Politics, and Postwork Imaginaries*, Durham, NC: Duke University Press.

Williamson, O. (1985) *The Economic Institutions of Capitalism*, New York: Free Press.

Wood, A. and Burchell, B. (2018) 'Unemployment and Well-Being', in A. Lewis (ed.), *The Cambridge Handbook of Psychology and Economic Behaviour*, Cambridge: Cambridge University Press, 234–59.

Woodcock, J. and Graham, M. (2020) *The Gig Economy: A Critical Introduction*, Cambridge: Polity.

Yeoman, R. (2014) 'Conceptualising Meaningful Work as a Fundamental Human Need', *Journal of Business Ethics*, 125: 235–51.

Index